A Song & Dance
For The North

The life story of a dedicated Northerner

Joe L Mills, OBE, DL

A Song & Dance For The North

The life story of
Joe L Mills, OBE, DL

With a foreword by
the Rt. Hon. Derek Foster, MP, DL

Little Egypt Publishing Ltd.

Printed and bound in Great Britain by intype London Ltd
Units 3/4 Elm Grove Industrial Estate, Elm Grove,
Wimbledon, SW19 4HE

Little Egypt Publishing Ltd
Sunderland
SR2 7BT

Front cover photograph by Trevor Craig

To my wife Lirena for her love, help, and understanding over the years, and for being a wonderful partner and mother to our daughters Joanne and Lucy

Acknowledgements

My thanks go to my biographer, Patrick Lavelle, to my friend George Craig, who inspired me to tell my story, to Paul Woods, for proofreading, to Trevor Craig, for the wonderful front cover photograph, to Jeremy Stephens, for picture layout , and, finally, to all my colleagues and friends within the Labour and trade union movement for their continued support.

Joe L Mills, 2002.

Foreword

Some pundits believe national politics has "switched off" many traditional Labour activists. Let us celebrate a "grass root", the son of a County Durham miner, who became very powerful in the Northern region, but remained an authentic voice of Labour.

Joe Mills may be a laugh a minute, with an endless fund of jokes and quips, which make him excellent company, but beneath this "song and dance" exterior beats the heart of a passionate politician.

Take regional government; the policy of the Northern Regional Labour Party since 1964. Joe Mills has been at the heart of the campaign for the last 25 years, fourteen of which he was Chairman of the Northern Regional Labour Party and Regional Secretary of the Transport and General Workers' Union. He commissioned much research to underpin the campaign and always pushed it to the top of the agenda.

When Labour came to power he was a founder member of the North East Constitutional Committee, to ensure the campaign was broadly based, as in Scotland.

At the height of his powers every Leader of the Labour Party, every MP and every candidate beat a path to his door because of the financial and organisational capacity of the T&GWU. I believe Tony Blair would not have become the MP for Sedgefield, without his intervention.

Joe was a consummate networker within the T&GWU and within the Labour Party nationally, but his skill was always used for the Labour Party in the North. No wonder the Northern Regional Labour Party punched well above its weight in those days!

Yet, he always used his power responsibly. For example Joe, together with Tom Burlison and Bob Howard, kept the trade unions and the Labour Party in the North "sensible" throughout the 1980s and early 1990s when the North West and London fell captive to the hard left.

Joe Mills was a founder member of the Northern Development Company, set up under a Tory government on a tripartite basis with the CBI, TUC and local government. It became the most powerful job-hunting agency in England and the forerunner of OneNorthEast. He was a member of the Tyne and Wear Development Corporation and the Port of Tyne Authority. He was on the Board of Governors at the University of Northumbria. He was Chairman of Priority Healthcare Wearside NHS Trust and then became Chairman of Sunderland Health Authority.

In all of these positions Joe used his organisational skills, first developed through the trade union movement. He never forgot his roots. Though still small in stature, he grew to walk tall by representing the people. He was highly respected by the business community because of his tough negotiating skills and his ability to deliver to his members.

His powerful position over 25 years, his sharp observational skills and his buoyant sense of humour, especially in adversity, give him a unique vantage point from which to comment as an authentic voice of the North.

Rt. Hon. Derek Foster, MP. DL.

Introduction

This is the life story of dedicated Northerner Joe Mills, who has spent more than 40 years in the trade union and Labour movement in England. Joe was one of the first leading Labour Party figures to press the case for regional government in the North. He was one of the men who helped put Tony Blair on the road to 10 Downing Street and the first leading union official to push for more democracy within the Labour Party through one member, one vote.

This story traces his life from his boyhood in the pit village of New Kyo, County Durham, to his Army days and his time as a leading union figure in the brewing industry.

It also follows his progress, and his eventual departure, from the Transport and General Workers' Union (T&GWU). It traces his links with leading North political figures such as T Dan Smith and Andrew Cunningham, and his efforts within his local Constituency Labour Party to weed out corruption.

The story also highlights his efforts to modernise the Labour Party, to attract inward investment to the North and his work on behalf of the T&GWU, all of which gave him three Honorary Degrees. It is a story of a man whose dedication and commitment to the North of England knows no bounds and of a man whose desire to see regional government in the North has earned him the nickname "Mr North".

Patrick Lavelle, 2002

Chapter One

THE square on his back was as black as the ace of spades; a black mark that appeared to be stuck to his lilywhite skin like a limpet. My father, Laurance Mills, was standing over the kitchen sink with a cut throat razor in his hand, dabbing soap on to his chin with a shaving brush. The fire in the front room was blazing as my mother, Mary, took hold of the poker and stabbed at the coal before placing the wet towel over the clothes stand and moving the stand in front of the fire.

"What's that black mark on my dad's back?" I asked, as mother picked the flannel from the blackened water in the tin bath and squeezed it as dry as she could.

"That's to strengthen your dad's back, Joe," my mother said. "You need to have a strong back, working down the pit."

My father washed the soap from his face and grabbed the steaming towel from the clothes stand, dabbing his chin and neck with it. "Let's get rid of this," he said, as he grabbed hold of one end of the tin bath while my mother grabbed the other.

Slowly, they manoeuvred their way through to the steep back stone stairs; my father, with arms outstretched, keeping the tin bath full of dirty water above his head. In the small yard, they stood, each holding one end of the bath. "After three", said my father, and after the count of three the water splashed on to the hard concrete of the back yard, most entering the drain, but some meandering its way through the grassed cracks of the uneven concrete.

Every night in Dudley Terrace, New Kyo, County Durham, was always bath night. My father would come home after his shift at Craghead Colliery thick with coal dust. Then it was out with the tin bath, which was placed in front of the fire in the living room, and the bath would be topped up with hot water from the boiler and cold water from a jug

I always had to leave the living room area, to give my father some privacy, but afterwards, when he was having a shave over the kitchen sink, with his braces hanging from his trousers, I couldn't help but stare at the black square on his back. One square of coal dust; that's all it was. And it was the same for many of my friend's fathers who also worked at the colliery face. If the square was washed off, according to local legend, the back would weaken and that could result in serious problems for the breadwinner in the family. The black patch was always washed off on a Friday night.

I liked Fridays. Not just because it was one day in the week when my father was not usually working a nightshift, which meant him leaving the house at midnight or even one o'clock in the morning, but it was also a day for treats and one when there was no need for me to raid the large pantry when I was suffering hunger pangs.

The small house was full of the mouthwatering aroma of pies being baked in the oven. There was never a great deal of money or food around during the week but come my father's pay day I knew mother would be baking us special treats; home-made meat and potato pies with apple pies to follow. We would sit around the blazing fire, and tuck in to my mother's specialities. It was always a welcome diversion from the toil and relative poverty of weekdays, when the pantry was virtually empty and the only constant in our lives was coal; coal my father hewed from the pit face and brought home on his body and clothes, and the concessionary coal which kept us warm, boiled our water, and filled the poss tub in which mother could wash the coal dust out of my father's clothes.

New Kyo was a typical pit village, between Annfield Plain and Stanley in Derwentside, County Durham, where the streets were very narrow and the back lanes narrower still. Tall wooden lamp-posts carried electricity to the very small houses in Dudley Terrace, where I spent the first few years of my life.

Our "house", these days, would be referred to as a flat, for it was nothing more than a number of upstairs rooms, the front door to which was reached by climbing some very steep stone steps. To the right of the front door, was a large sink with one cold water tap; our only source of water. Next to the sink was a large bench which my mother used for everything from washing dishes to baking pies. To the left, there was a fireplace with a boiler, to boil all the hot water we needed.

In the living room, the large open fire had an oven at either end for cooking and near the fire, surrounded by an old brass fender, there was always a box or something similar where the sticks to light the fire were stored.

We'd sit around the fire on cold winter Friday nights eating our pies, feeling the benefit of the heat on our legs, listening to the wireless, and my parents would chat to each other or any one of our regular visitors.

The house was very sparsely furnished and the only floor covering was oil cloth and a large "clippy" mat, made up of clippings or bits of material pressed into hessian. Like the black square on a pitman's back, the clippy mat was something peculiar not just to New Kyo, but to most of the pit villages dotted around the North East.

The furniture was ordinary. We had a large three piece suite, a large table to eat from, another bit of furniture that looked like an old sewing machine and a radio. The house had two bedrooms, one occupied by my mother and father and one occupied by me, but as a very young boy I would sleep between my parents in their bed just to keep warm.

Like my father, I too would have a bath in front of the big open fire but, occasionally, I would bathe in my mother's poss tub. She used a type of washing powder, which, if I remember rightly, was called Dolly Blue, and she would beat the dirt out of the clothes with a poss stick. I would jump into the poss tub when the washing was done and have a good, hot, soak in the soapy water. And when I was done, I'd dry myself down with a towel in front of the open fire and notice my skin had a distinct blue hue to it. The blue tint didn't last very long, and wouldn't have done me any harm, I was told.

A family called Simpson lived in the house below us at number 13 Dudley Terrace and we shared two things with the Simpson family; the back yard and the only outside toilet. We each had our own coalhouse in the yard.

Most of the houses in New Kyo had an outside toilet, nettie, or midden and the narrowness of the streets meant it was difficult for the wagons to gain access to deliver coal or empty the outside loos.

The rows of houses backed on to each other, separated by a back lane that could have been no more than ten feet wide, and at the rear of all of the houses was a hatch covered with a wooden door which allowed people to shovel coal from the lane straight into the coalhouse. The concessionary coal was always just dumped in the lane outside the miners' homes and, on a dry day, that created problems. Miners' wives, after a heavy shift with the poss tub, would have hung out their clothes (with a hint of Dolly Blue) on the washing line in their small back yards only to discover later that the washing was covered in a thin layer of coal dust after a delivery to a neighbour who had been hard at work shovelling the coal into the coal house. There were many, many, rows among neighbours in the street.

The men of New Kyo, like the men of nearby Stanley, Consett, South Moor, Annfield Plain, and the scores of other pit villages dotted around this area of County Durham, worked at the pits, the brickyards, Consett Ironworks, or didn't work at all.

Sons followed fathers and their fathers before them down the pits, into the brickworks or the ironworks, not that they didn't know any other, it was perhaps that they didn't want to know any other. In the pit villages there was a very strong sense of tradition; a kind of uniformity, a sense of being comfortable with the familiar.

The houses in New Kyo were much of a muchness; small, sparsely furnished, with shared yards and shared loos, all with a similar lay out, all with the same amount of living space. Enter one house in Dudley Terrace and another in Woodbine Terrace and there would be little difference between the two.

But there was one peculiarity to the houses in New Kyo and that was all of the gates and doors on the homes which had been repaired over the years were a different colour, possibly painted with paint taken from one of the brickyards. Perhaps this one exception to the norm gave each of the families their own sense of individual identity. Or perhaps the differing coloured gates and doors was to ensure the occupants entered the right house.

The houses in New Kyo were, generally, in a dilapidated state. The villagers were generally poor, eking out an existence from day to day. The houses were generally in a poor state of repair, the narrow roads full of potholes; there was a stench in the air from the outside toilets, and the atmosphere was always choked with smoke or coal dust.

This was New Kyo, County Durham, and it was where myself and my family called home.

Chapter Two

The tradition in most mining families, where sons follow in their fathers footsteps to work in the pits, was a common tradition in County Durham pit villages and so it was with my family. My grandfather, Laurance Mills, was a miner in Burnhope and my father, also called Laurance, worked in Craghead Colliery and later South Moor Colliery.

The Mills' family tree, however, is far from traditional or conventional, with second marriages, step brothers and sisters and even a step grandfather not unheard of. In later life I learned that my grandmother and grandfather did not get married until they were 67 years old!

I was born on December 16th, 1934, in the Princess Mary Maternity Home in Newcastle Upon Tyne. My mother Mary was only a small woman and had to be admitted to the Newcastle Maternity Home because of fears there may be complications with my birth. Fortunately, that did not happen.

My grandfather's first wife died, leaving him with two children Lilian and William, and a few years later he remarried. His bride was a woman named Elizabeth Brown, and they had three children of their own; my father Laurance, my uncle Joseph and my aunt Ellen.

A few years after the death of my grandfather, Elizabeth met and married Thomas "Bocker" McHale, who was from the Trimdon area of County Durham. He was known as Bocker

– a version of boxer – because he was a well-known bareknuckle streetfighter who made quite a lot of money going around the pubs and clubs of County Durham challenging all-comers. Bocker McHale was also something of a waster who liked more than a few drinks and his marriage to my grandmother Elizabeth, was looked upon as something of an unholy alliance, as she was a Salvationist.

My grandmother and Bocker McHale were married in 1915 and she died from tuberculosis in 1930, leaving Bocker with five children (my father, uncle Joe, aunt Ellen and Lilian and William from my grandmother's first marriage). None of the children were Bocker's own.

My mother Mary's parents were Joe and Annie Bell, whose maiden name was George. Annie had five brothers, Robert, David, Joe, Thomas and the youngest Jimmy, as well as one sister, Mary, who all lived at Oxhill, near Stanley, County Durham. Young Jimmy was always very close to his sister Annie (my grandmother on my mother's side) and lived with her virtually all of his life.

My mother Mary also had a sister who was very close to our family, Margaret Georgina, known affectionately to me as Aunt Meggie. Aunt Meggie visited our house in New Kyo regularly.

At the top of our street stood a corner shop run by a woman called Francis, who always wore black. She sold everything from sweets to flour and allowed the poverty stricken wives of the village to run up credit each week, paying the bill on pay day. Another corner shop opened opposite but did not survive long; there was not enough money in New Kyo to sustain two corner shops selling virtually the same items.

Opposite the corner shop was Thorn's fish shop. Fish and chips was a regular meal for the people of New Kyo and they would queue regularly for their suppers; a cod lot, a pattie lot, or just a bag of chips, but always with plenty of batter

Around the corner from the fish shop was the local workingmens' club, The Central, and every man locally was a member. At the weekends, the talk was about how much coal had been produced at the local colliery that week, how much money they had made, and how much cash they had kept back from their wives.

The Sunday afternoon pint at the club was another age-old tradition in New Kyo, tolerated by the long-suffering wives, as was a couple of hours' sleep after the afternoon session.

Down from the club was the Miners' Institute, which was a very large hall with an auditorium and a stage, where many local showgroups would perform.

Downstairs there was a billiard hall with three tables. But I wasn't allowed to go in there. My father always believed that anyone who was good at snooker or billiards had had a mis-spent youth.

The personal poverty and the collective economic deprivation of New Kyo as a village appeared to act as a bonding agent for the local residents. They were a clannish lot and there was a real sense of community, with a strong emphasis on clean living and the family.

One family called Hole, I remember well. The father Jimmy Hole and his wife Brenda brought up 13 children in a house with only two small bedrooms. I remember going in the house one day when they were having tea and I was asked to sit by the fire until they had finished. They were all drinking out of jam jars.

Whenever anyone was in difficulty in the village there was always other people who could be relied on. The children all used to go out mushroom and blackberry picking, or out chopping sticks and selling them around the doors.

At the age of four-and-a-half, I moved with my family to South Moor, a pit village not far from New Kyo, into an upstairs two-bedroomed house at number 11 Mitchell Street. The house was very similar to the one in Dudley Terrace, though it appeared smaller to me. As well as the two small bedrooms there was a living room and a scullery and, in the rear yard, an outside toilet and a coal house. I couldn't understand why it was we had to move initially, but it became clearer when my step-grandfather Bocker McHale started to lodge with us.

Bocker was very much left on his own when the family went their separate ways and my father felt obliged to provide accommodation for him. Bocker had some form of injury and every other day the district nurse called to dress a very large open wound in his right shoulder. I was never sure how Bocker had come by his injury. I would watch the nurse tend to his wound and think how very painful it must have been for Bocker. With my young and wild imagination I thought maybe Bocker had suffered the wound in a very violent bare-knuckle street fight or that perhaps he had been shot.

A few months after we moved, Bocker left the home in Mitchell Street and went into hospital in South Moor. I was never told why. But he died and was buried from our home, though I did not attend his funeral. My father kept the bill for the funeral; 10 shillings and sixpence.

With Bocker McHale gone, there was only my father, mother and myself left in this old house in South Moor, which was a problem as we were away from my grandmother, Annie Bell and my Aunt Meggie in New Kyo. Whenever we went to visit them it was a long walk up the Black Road up to New Kyo, when the weather was good. Otherwise, we would catch a bus.

At the top of Mitchell Street, there was a large green shed in front of a dirt track on the road leading up to Ox Hill, south of New Kyo. This green shed was the corner shop and it sold everything imaginable.

Next door to the shop, about ten yards away, was Dr Fox's surgery, which I visited from time to time with the normal childhood ailments.

South Moor was different in many ways to New Kyo, but in other ways very similar. Its main street had shops either side, including a newsagent's and an ice cream shop called Bovey's. Then there was McHale's the barbers. My father was a bit of barber himself. He used to cut friends' and neighbours' hair in the back yard while they sat on a stool. I recall him cutting my hair.

My dad was a member of the Territorial Army, company of the 8th Battalion, which was based at Stanley, no more than a mile away from New Kyo and South Moor. He attended the TA on Tuesday and Thursday evenings and always looked extremely smart in his uniform. Sometimes, he went away with the TA on weekend camps. He attained the rank of Sergeant and the small amount of cash he was paid for his services in the TA helped to supplement the family income.

In his neatly pressed uniform, with the three stripes on his arms, his peaked cap and his highly-polished boots, I would look at my father walking, almost marching, to catch his bus from South Moor to Stanley twice a week. On his return, I would normally be tucked up in bed asleep.

However, on one Thursday night when he returned from Stanley, my mother woke me up and led me into the living room where my father was sitting in his armchair, his peaked cap in his hands, with a look of sorrow on his face.

"Your father and I have something to tell you, Joe," my mother said looking equally forlorn.

"What is it mam?" I asked innocently.

My father took hold of me by the arms, pulled me to his chest and embraced me. I could see his eyes glistening with tears.

"I have to go away son," he said. "But I won't be away for long and I'll write to you and your mother as often as I can."

"Where are you going dad?" I asked.

"Your dad's going to war, Joe," my mother said. "He's going to fight for our country and we can both be very proud of him."

In early 1940, at the age of five, I couldn't really understand what was going on. But I knew there was a lot of sadness in our house that night. My mother tucked me up in bed and bid me goodnight. She looked worried.

There were several other men in South Moor, New Kyo, and surrounding villages, who were members of the Territorial Army, and, like hundreds of part-time reservists across Great Britain, they were among the first called into the conflict.

A few days later, I watched as my father put on his familiar uniform and packed his kit bag. He led me down to the street and we waited on the street corner. An Army wagon pulled up, my father gave me one last embrace, got on board and waved as the wagon pulled away.

My mother was able to go to the drill hall at Stanley, along with other wives and girlfriends, to bid their husbands or partners a formal farewell. But for me, the last I saw of my father in 1940 was him waving from the back of the Army wagon as it left South Moor, heading for something I did not understand ... war.

Chapter Three

I stood on top of the overturned pop bottle crate, took the small baton in my hand, and struck up the band at the Miners' Welfare Hall in New Kyo. I moved the baton up and down in a triangular motion, and with each small twist of this little baton the hall reverberated to the sound of music. For a boy, aged five or six, the ability to strike up the band with nothing more than a little stick, and to appear to keep the beat going, was nothing short of magical. I was dressed in a small, authentic-looking lieutenant's uniform my mother had had specially made for me at Isaac Walton the tailor's in Newcastle. As the little soldier boy I was really in my element, revelling in all the attention and soaking up the limelight. At such an early age I had discovered something that I enjoyed immensely, and something that would stay with me for the rest of my life ... the art of showmanship.

The Saturday night dancing at the Miners' Hall was organised by the Miners' Institute, for miners not obliged to go to the war and their wives and the wives of servicemen. On a Saturday night in New Kyo, it was the place to be. My mother, Aunt Meggie and other members of the family took me along to the Miners' Hall on dance nights. For me, it was the highlight of the week.

I had started to go to the dance hall a few weeks earlier with my mother and I gazed at the activity with a sense of wonderment and fascination. It was all a far cry from the daily grind in the pit villages and the worry about the men at war. In the hall people seemed to come to life.

Only two days after my father left for war, I had been playing outside the shop, the old shed, at the top of the street in South Moor, running around with friends, when I tripped in a pothole and fractured my skull. I don't recall much about the accident itself other than a number of people around me looking anxious and the terrible pain searing through my body.

I was carried into a house on the corner of the street and my mother and Dr Fox were sent for. Dr Fox was able to stem the blood and apply a number of clips to the wound but nothing seemed to have been done about the fracture itself, because all the way through my life I carried a dent in the top of my skull.

I developed a mild form of pneumonia and for several weeks I was in and out of hospital, drifting in and out of consciousness. Unknown to me, my father, at that stage based at Catterick, North Yorkshire, had been told about my accident and was given a day's compassionate leave. He came and sat by my hospital bedside, but I never came round during the short time he was there. I wouldn't see my father for another six or so years.

My father, my mother learned after a few months, had been captured at the beginning of the war in Poland and was to spend the rest of the conflict as a prisoner of war.

Only a few weeks after my father went to the war, my mother and I moved back to New Kyo, to number two Catherine Terrace, which was one street down from Dudley Terrace, where we had lived before the move to South Moor, and only a street away from Percy Terrace, where my grandmother lived with my Uncle Jimmy.

The house in Catherine Terrace was a corner house and had one bedroom, a living room and an enclosed staircase.

We shared the back yard with a Mr Robson who lived

downstairs, an elderly gentleman with a sharp red face and a miserable demeanour who rarely exchanged the time of day with us. There was an outside netty and a coal house.

Around the corner, there was a fruiterers, run by a man called Mr Carrick, who was a special constable. He was a very large gentleman and I felt rather comfortable that he lived there. He looked impressive in his uniform. I suppose living alone with my mother next to a policeman did give me some feeling of security, with my father away at war.

Next door to the fruiterers was a clothes shop and further up the street was a post office and milliner's, owned by a Mr Hetherington, who was always referred to locally as Mr Conchy. At the time, I didn't know why he was given that nickname but learned later that it was because he was a conscientious objector.

Down the street, opposite my grandmother's house, was a butcher's shop called Castle's, which had a very large yard. I would often see a van pull up with live pigs in the back. The animals would end up hanging in the front window for sale. I went off eating meat for quite a while after my first sight of the pigs. Right next door to the butcher's shop was a shop run by a Mr Fitzpatrick, a herbalist known for his strange remedies and his very large moustache. My mother preferred his medical remedies to those dispensed by Dr Fox.

With my grandmother and grandfather Joe living in New Kyo, no more than a street away, it was obvious to me that my mother and I had returned home, even though the house we were living in was a different address to our previous home in the village. My Uncle Jimmy had lodged with my grandparents for several years. Jimmy was my grandmother's youngest brother.

Jimmy had worked in Coventry and different parts of the country but was now working in a local brickyard. His favourite meal was a couple of fresh eggs with as many slices of bread he could eat. My mother kept him supplied with as much as she could. He was an extremely good eater at any time.

Two doors' away from my grandmother, in Percy Terrace, at number 18, was my dad's brother, Joe Mills, who had married Suzie Gent. She had two children, Kevin and Derek, by a previous marriage. Derek ended up in approved school and was never seen much around New Kyo. When Suzie married my Uncle Joe, they later had two children of their own, Ronnie and John.

Although they lived close to us, for some reason I wasn't encouraged to visit Uncle Joe very often, though I did go to see him. He had an allotment near the house where he would breed hens. Ronnie, the oldest son from my Uncle Joe's second marriage, was often spotted coming down from the allotment with fresh eggs and other things in his bucket.

On the corner of Catherine Terrace was a barber's shop and I used to stand outside, looking in the window watching the barber at work and remembering my father cutting hair in the back yard. I missed my father.

Up the road from the barber's shop was the real focal point of the community, the Miners' Hall, with its large stage, downstairs reading rooms and snooker tables and, at the rear of the building, a very large swimming pool, used years earlier by the miners but now in a dilapidated state.

My mother sometimes attended the Saturday night dances at the miners' hall without me, which disappointed me once I had been bitten by the showmanship bug as the little soldier conducting the band. But the hall was only 50 yards or so from our house. I was locked in the warm house, and no harm was to come to me.

One night, after we had been at Catherine Terrace for a few months, my mother and I got ready and she said she was taking me three streets away to see a Mrs Effie Wilson who ran a show group. My mother seemed to think that as I liked standing up in the hall and conducting the band that I might want to join the showgroup, and that might put me on the early road into showbusiness. I wasn't sure at the time what the showgroup was, but I thought it was a good idea.

We walked through the streets of New Kyo in the dark and my mother knocked on the front door of the home of Mrs Effie Wilson. This rather larger-than-life lady opened the door and welcomed us in. It was obvious from their conversation that my mother had spoken to her beforehand. We went into a large room in the back of the house, where Mrs Wilson did her teaching.

There was about a dozen pupils sitting around and at the back end of the room there was a curtain which was a makeshift stage used for practising. I noticed she had a son called Carl, but he never got involved in the showgroup.

My mother left me at the house and I was to be taken through the rudiments of dancing. Almost 60 years before the son of a miner, Billy Elliot, from a North East colliery village, hit the big screen as the only boy in a dancing school full of girls, here I was, little Joe Mills, the son of a miner, the only boy in a dancing class in a North East pit village ... full of girls.

I remember standing with my hand resting on the back of a chair trying to work out which was my right foot and which was my left.

"Stamp, shuffle, stamp," said Mrs Effie Wilson.

"Stamp, shuffle, stamp," she said, as I tried to keep up with the girls.

I attended these dance classes every Tuesday and Thursday evening and my mother was so encouraged by the progress I had made she took me down to a local shop one day to buy me a pair of tap shoes. The shoes were quite a novelty, but I thought they

27

were a little cissyfied, what with them being shiny patent leather with taps fitted on both the heel and the toe.

At the time, I did wonder whether my enjoyment of dancing would be frowned upon by my male friends in New Kyo, but I was soon to be hit by a revelation that would dispel in one fell swoop any concerns I might have had about being a "cissy" dancer. It came one night at my grandmother's house in the large shape of my Uncle Jimmy – all 20 stone of him.

I was sitting by the fire, watching the flames dancing around the hearth, when Uncle Jimmy came home after a hard day's graft at the brickyard.

Jimmy sat down next to me by the fire, while my grandmother went to the corner shop to buy his tea; three eggs and a mountain of bread and butter.

"Have you got your tap shoes?" Jimmy asked.

"Yes," I said, moving to the cupboard where the shiny, new, black, patent leather shoes were stored.

I handed the shoes to my Uncle Jimmy, along with the taps that had yet to be nailed into the soles. He took hold of them and pulled a penknife from his pocket and slowly carved a square of rubber from the heels, about half-an-inch deep. I'd never seen Uncle Jimmy in such deep concentration.

When the holes in the heels were carved, Jimmy dipped his hand into his trouser pocket and pulled out four farthings, placing two in the hole in the heel he had carved in each shoe. He then got hold of the cobbler's last, stored in the scullery cupboard, and nailed the tap plates to the heels and the tap plates to the front of the shoes.

"There you go," said my Uncle Jimmy. "Your shoes can tap, but they can also jingle, and when you're on stage people will look, and they'll listen."

He passed me the shoes and I looked at his handiwork and my Uncle Jimmy went back into the scullery, came back into the living room, took off his working boots, put on a pair of wooden clogs, stood up and started dancing. This mountain of a man, who was as deep as the Indian Ocean, was as nimble on his feet as Rudolph Nureyev in his prime.

His face lit up, his heavy, wooden clogs beat out the rhythm of his soul, and for the first time in my life, I saw a man transformed. Only then did I learn that my modest and unassuming Uncle Jimmy had been the Northern Regional Clog Dancing Champion.

At the tender age of almost six I was embarking upon a new career as a dancer and my Uncle Jimmy, who spoke in a whisper when anyone else was around, was the most inspirational teacher I could have hoped for. For the rudiments of dancing and the practical know-how, I always had Mrs Effie Wilson. But when I turned up at her classes and started the "stamp, shuffle, stamp" routine, Mrs Wilson, and the rest of the class, realised my feet were not just dancing, they were singing.

Over the next few months other dancers came to the classes with jingling feet. Mrs Wilson told us we were to perform in public for the first time; six venues had been lined up around the area for the charity shows. The first show was called Sweet Angeline, which was all about a young man and a young woman getting married and all the other things that marriage entailed. One of the main parts was that of the groom. With only one boy in the showgroup, that main part could only go to one boy – little Joe Mills with his jingling feet.

Chapter Four

Arriving home after a day at school, I noticed the furniture in the front room of our small house in Catherine Terrace had been moved around. In a corner of the room, two small beds had been erected and there was a small screen around them.

I was surprised to see the silhouette of a man sitting in an armchair in front of the fire and, at first, I wondered whether my father had managed to escape from the prisoner of war camp to come home.

My mother told me the stranger was a Bevan Boy, who had come to live with us. She had registered with the National Coal Board for two miners who had volunteered to work in the pits rather than go to war.

About an hour later, another chap appeared who was extremely well-spoken and turned out to be from London and had worked in the city. The other worked in a chocolate factory in Slough.

These were the first two Bevan Boys I met, but over the next two of three years many came and went. Our house was so small we were almost tripping over each other, and, for me, the arrival of the Bevan Boys was nothing more than inconvenient. It did provide my mother, though, with a little extra income.

Prior to taking in the Bevan Boys, my mother had worked for some time in the munitions factory in Gateshead along with other women, to help the war effort and to make some money.

This didn't work out very well at all, as my grandmother had to look after me and it was making my mother very tired.

The domestic situation wasn't ideal at all, but at least I still had the showgroup to look forward to and my grandmother's house to visit just around the corner from us

The showgroup's first show was at the New Kyo Miners' Hall and it was crowded to capacity. Charity shows at the time were few and far between. My grandmother and all of the family were there along with neighbours. I thoroughly enjoyed being one of the stars of the show, very much in the limelight. It was quite an experience and gave me quite a buzz, particularly the applause at the end. I felt so proud when my mother told everyone how "brilliant" I had done. She said that I really should try to make a career on the stage.

In lots of the shows around the pit villages in the North East we changed the show from time to time and there was always a major part for the male, which shot me into the limelight. I enjoyed the shows but found myself getting tired. They ran from 7pm up to about 10 pm, which meant having to get a bus back to my home. While I was only seven or eight, I still felt it was having some effect on me. Because of all the singing I also had problems with sore throats. I had to go to see the local doctor who was very sympathetic. Knowing I was doing a lot of work for charity, I would receive treatment without any cost.

Apart from the organised shows, I was often requested by charities to do a turn at various places and I ended up going to organisations such as the National Institution for the Blind and to residential homes for the elderly.

All the activity with the regular shows and the extra shows I was involved in for charity was taxing my strength and my grandmother indicated that I should really slow down – slow down, I thought, at the tender age of eight. My role in the showgroup was certainly getting me noticed and I was hardly able to walk through Annfield Plain, Stanley, South Moor or New Kyo, without being recognised as young Joe Mills from the showgroup.

I started school at Annfield Plain School and had a short period of schooling at South Moor. At Annfield Plain Infants' School, I was with a lot of children who I already knew from New Kyo and others from Annfield Plain.

One particular school project involved writing a story about where our parents lived and indicating where our fathers were at the time. All the material was to be made up into a montage for the classroom wall.

Many of the children wrote of how their fathers were digging coal down the pit, driving or working in brickyards. There were about 30 pupils but there were only four soldiers on the montage and one of them was my father. I had to draw a picture of my father and when I did I made sure I got the three stripes on his arm, which made me very proud.

The three other soldiers, it turned out, were at Catterick or some other British base. My father was the only PoW featured on the class montage. I would often look at the pictures on the wall and wonder what my father was doing, whether he was safe, when he might come home. It made me sad, and this was noticed by the class teacher, a Mrs Broadbent, who would often ask me if I had heard any news about my father.

At one stage, about two years later, he was reported missing presumed dead but my mother later received a letter from the War Office saying he was a now PoW in Bavaria.

With so much activity in our small house, what with the comings and goings of the Bevan Boys, I was spending more and more time with the showgroup and a lot of time with my grandmother, just a few doors away, where I would be given more tuition from my clog dancing champion Uncle Jimmy.

My mother encouraged me in other directions as well as the

showgroup. I joined the St Aidan's Church Choir in Annfield Plain. To join, I had to sing to the choirmaster who would judge whether I had a good enough voice. I sang Onward Christian Soldiers but as I sang it, in true showmanship style, I moved my arms around as if it was a rendition. The bandmaster stopped halfway through and told me I was not on the stage. He told me to sing it and keep my hands by my sides.

I attended choir practice on a Monday and Friday evenings and church on a Sunday morning and Sunday School on the afternoon. It was back to church on Sunday night. With all that going on every week and my heavy involvement with the showgroup, from the age of six to eleven I had a very busy and active young life. Thankfully, I don't think my schoolwork suffered.

At the age of 11, I sat the 11 plus but, despite my teachers predicting I would sail through the exam, I failed, so would not be heading to Stanley Grammar School.

There was a lot happening in my life leading up to the exam that year. My Aunt Meggie had moved from Annfield Plain to 20 Percy Terrace in New Kyo. My grandmother moved from 20 Percy Terrace to a smaller house in Woodbine Terrace, along with my Uncle Jimmy, whose bed was tucked into an alcove. I spent a lot of time at my grandmother's house and felt comfortable with her and my Uncle Jimmy.

Whenever I slept overnight at my grandmother's, I'd sleep in a small corner bed she arranged in the room and there was as paraffin lamp in the corner on top of the dressing table. If I felt cold, frightened or uncomfortable, I would creep into my grandmother's large, high, bed for the night.

There was a curtain over the alcove to give Uncle Jimmy some privacy. It was small but comfortable house. Every Saturday morning my mother or Aunt Meggie would come up to clean the hearth and black-lead the fire.

Things seemed quite normal at our family home in Catherine

Terrace. My mother was always busy organising meals for the Bevan Boys. Every six months or so, two of them would leave to be replaced by two more. I had some interesting conversations with the Bevan Boys. What with me being so young and never having ventured anywhere other than Stanley, Annfield Plain, South Moor or New Kyo, finding out where they lived and something about their lives, even if they just came from the Midlands, was something new to me.

One particular Bevan Boy called Peter was a very interesting character. He was from Oldham in Lancashire and he told me his parents had a shop in Manchester Street where they sold clothes. I assumed from that, that he was quite well off. He also told me about his brother Billy, who he said was a professional boxer, and this intrigued me as I was interested in boxing and would often listen to the bouts on the wireless. Peter told me his brother was a middleweight and met many of the stars of the day. I was quite impressed.

One day at the house in Catherine Terrace my mother asked me to go on an important errand.

"Joe," she said. "I'd like you to take this letter to the Post Office in Annfield Plain, and make sure you post it properly."

"Why can't I post it in New Kyo?" I asked.

"Because I want you to post it in Annfield Plain", my mother said.

The letter was one of the special types; a blue air mail letter which folded into an envelope, which were given special status by the Post Office. When my mother wrote to my father the letters were all posted in New Kyo.

In New Kyo, I stood at the stop waiting for the bus to Annfield Plain and the contents of the blue envelope was tearing a hole in my conscience. I knew it had to be important, I knew it was a letter written by my mother to my father, but what did it say? Why was it so important that I post this one letter in

Annfield Plain, a bus ride away from New Kyo?

I took the envelope from my jacket pocket, held it in front of my eyes, read the address, put it back in my pocket, pulled it out again, and wrestled with my conscience.

I opened the letter.

As I read the words my eyes were filled with the kind of tears that burn; the kind of tears that sting.

My mother was telling my father that she wanted a divorce; that she had never seen him for four years and they had grown apart; that she couldn't bear being apart from him and that she needed to find a relationship to keep her sanity. She said she hoped he would understand.

I was gobsmacked.

The bus for Annfield Plain arrived and I got on, sobbing and rubbing my eyes and hoping that the other passengers wouldn't notice. I couldn't bear to think of the impact such devastating news would have on my father, living out the war years in a PoW camp.

At Annfield Plain I got off the bus and walked to the post office. Should I post it? I asked myself. If I don't post it, will my father return home after the war? It was a thorny dilemma I had brought upon myself by opening the letter. It really was too much for a ten-year-old boy. I stood at the post office for a lot longer than I had intended and, eventually, put the blue envelope into the post box.

As it left my hand I still didn't know whether I was doing the right thing. Instead of getting the bus back to New Kyo, which was about a mile and a half away, I decided to walk, and it was quite a distance.

On the way home, I wondered what was going to happen in the future. I thought about telling my mother I had read the letter, or telling my grandmother what I knew.

But, for now, I decided, it was something I shouldn't mention. For the next few weeks, I carried this dark secret around with me, and it ate into my thoughts almost every hour.

The biggest worry I had, was whether or not I would see my father again.

Chapter Five

The shock on my grandmother's face as I peeped through the door to the living room of her home was very apparent to me, but why she looked in such a state, I didn't know. I pushed the door open a little wider, and there, at the dining table, sat my mother, Aunt Meggie and Peter the Bevan Boy, all with equally concerned expressions on their faces.

"Is that you Joe?" My grandmother asked, as I entered the room. I had just been playing in the street with friends and was rather excitable, though my mood changed dramatically when I saw my grandmother, mother, Aunt Meggie and Peter sitting around the table.

"Come and sit down Joe," my grandmother said. She then turned to my mother and said: "I think you had better tell little Joe now what this is all about".

The dark secret was out and the reason for my mother's request for a divorce became all too clear. She had been having an affair with Peter and they planned to move to his home town of Oldham.

I was more shocked then than I was when I opened the blue envelope before posting it in Annfield Plain. I didn't fully understand just what was going on.

"You don't have to move to Oldham, if you don't want to Joe," my grandmother said. "You can stay here with me and your Uncle Jimmy."

What with my father having been away in a PoW camp, and with me not having seen him in more than four years, I didn't want to lose my mother.

The shock of what was going on and being talked about sunk in, and I burst into tears. After a few minutes, we all sat down to talk about the situation. My grandmother, my Aunt Meg and Uncle Jimmy were totally opposed to the whole idea of my mother moving to Oldham, and made it plain. My mother was equally as determined to move away.

"I think the world of Peter and I want to live with him," my mother said.

"We've thought long and hard about it, and we think it would be best if we moved to Oldham."

I didn't want to move to Lancashire and said so, but my mother suggested that she and Peter would move there first, set up home, and come back for me. By that time, I will have decided whether I wanted to stay with my grandmother in New Kyo or move away.

A few weeks later, my mother sold off all of her possessions in Catherine Terrace and gave her key up to her landlord and departed for Oldham. I went to spend the next few weeks living with my grandmother.

At the age of 11, this was the fifth house I had lived in. I liked living with my grandmother, she made a terrible fuss of me. Every morning she would send me off to school after a nice breakfast. There was always a large fire in the hearth and in the evenings we spent a lot of time listening to musical programmes on the wireless, particularly the old song and dance men at the Palace of Varieties. It was a very happy time for me. I wondered how my mother was getting on, though she did write quite regularly. I didn't understand why she chose to do what she did, but it was her decision. It made me very sad at the time. Quite often I would lie in my bed at my grandmother's house and think about my dad in Poland, my mother in Oldham, and my own situation in New Kyo.

Fortunately, for me, I still had the showgroup and the church choir. I still had a lot of things going on without two parents to guide me. Although it was a sad time for me, I thanked God that my grandmother was and my Uncle Jimmy were around to give me the security and the comfort that I craved.

Some weeks after my mother left for Oldham we received a letter from her to say she was coming home for a few days, hopefully to take me back to Oldham to live with her and Peter. I was excited at seeing my mother again, but I wasn't looking forward to the prospect of moving to Oldham. My grandmother said if I didn't want to go my mother wouldn't force me. Particularly, because of my schooling.

When my mother appeared, we were all pleased to see her. We sat around the table and she spoke of a good life she was making for herself with Peter in Oldham.

During the next few days, while she stayed she convinced me I should join her. I wasn't too sure I was doing the right thing.

I was torn between staying with my grandmother, who had cared for me so well, and moving away with my mother to a strange house in a strange town, living with a man I hardly knew.

My mother was very persuasive and, a couple of days later, I packed my bags and caught the bus with my mother to Newcastle to get the train. The train journey was quite exciting because I never had been on a train for such a long journey. We went through a few towns I had heard of but never visited. We arrived in Manchester and had to get another train to Oldham.

At the Oldham station we were met by Peter, who was very pleased to see us. I was moving into my sixth house in ten years. The house wasn't far from the railway station, near St Mary's Church in the town. I noticed people walking along the road with clogs on, which I thought was very strange. Clogs, like my Uncle

Jimmy's clogs, I thought, were for dancing, not for wearing every day. My mother told me that a lot of people in Oldham wore clogs every day. They worked in cotton mills around the town. I also noticed a lot of people had shawls around their heads and shoulders. It was all so foreign to me, but would have amused my friends in New Kyo, I thought.

When we arrived at the house I would be living in at the top of the street, the picture painted to me by Peter, and to some extent my mother, about life in Oldham had been made out far rosier than it actually was. The house was very sparsely furnished, though my mother said they were saving to buy more furniture for the rooms.

After a tea and scone, Peter and my mother and I went to see his brother; the middleweight boxing champion who knew a lot of the stars. We knocked at the door and went into the house. It was one of the worst houses that I had ever seen; in a far worse state than even the most dilapidated house in New Kyo.

Alarm bells started ringing in my head. The stories Peter had told me about his successful boxing brother, the family's clothes shop in Manchester Street, and all the other stories about the good life in Oldham, just didn't hold true.

We went back to our house and after a meal of pie and peas – which seemed a traditional meal – we went to see Peter's mother and father in Manchester Street. The clothes shop was indeed a clothes shop; it was a second hand shop that had seen far better days.

Within a few hours of my arrival in Oldham, I began to question whether I had made the right decision. I was also concerned about whether my mother had made the right decision in coming to live here. Peter's mother and father were very old and didn't seem very warm towards me or my mother. I got the impression they disapproved of the relationship.

I looked around the house and found it had one bedroom, a scullery, a small living room and a camp bed in the corner which I had to sleep in. There was a coke fire in the living room, giving out a lot of heat, but once the fire went out it cooled very quickly and the living room became quite cold.

I went to bed and tried to close my eyes. Outside, a gas lamp shone brightly into the house and every half hour the chimes of St Mary's Church clock rang out loud and true.

The next morning, we had a conversation about school and when I would like to start. I was also told my father had been released from the PoW Camp and was back in the UK, working in Dover with the repatriated prisoners, helping them with their release. It was obvious to me why he had stayed in Dover, because my mother had given up her home and there was nowhere for him to stay other than at his sister's in Dudley Terrace, New Kyo. It seemed obvious to me that my mother had wanted me away from New Kyo just in case I had any contact with my father.

I didn't understand why she did this and I was confused, but I decided to try and get on with life in Oldham. I started school and made few, if any, friends. The pupils stared at me in the schoolyard as if I was a foreigner in their midst.

One girl, Beatrice Barnes, known as BB, did speak to me. She said her grandparents had lived in the North East for some time. But she had the mickey taken out of her by the rest of the class for befriending me. I found it difficult to understand the accents of the children and I am sure they had the same difficulty understanding me.

Over the weeks ahead, I longed to be back in New Kyo and at Annfield Plain School. I moped around the house a lot, then joined the choir at St Mary's Church after my mother suggested it would do me good.

In Oldham there was very little money around, and the lack of cash and food on the table caused constant rows between my mother and Peter. Their apparent love for each other was being tested to the limit. We had to wait until pay day on the Friday to get the groceries in to have a decent meal, which was usually pies and peas.

My mother had to take a job as a cleaner in an antiquated solicitor's office in the town and started at 6am, lighting three fires in the building in time for the staff arriving.

I felt sorry for her, having to get up so early, so I started going to the offices with her on a morning, to keep her company and to try to lift her dampened spirits. Without Peter around, we had some open and frank discussions and I detected that all wasn't well with the relationship between my mother and him.

After cleaning the offices, we would pop into a local cafe for tea and toast and my mother would then walk me to school, where I would have to again endure the unfriendly atmosphere and the staring eyes and grinning faces of the children who saw me as an outsider.

Peter worked at the local mill but appeared to be at home more times than he was at work. When the very sore subject of money reared its head, he would fly into a violent temper, clashing doors and shouting, then brooding for hours on end.

His temper frightened me. It wasn't something I had witnessed in New Kyo. My mother said it was just his way of venting his frustration over the lack of money coming into the house.

Inevitably, it all came to a head one day when my mother flew into an uncontrollable rage. Peter started shouting loudly, then picked up a dining room chair and smashed it on the floor. He then picked up other pieces of furniture and did the same, before walking through the door and slamming it shut hard.

I broke down and cried and so did my mother. She then ushered me into the bedroom and pulled two small, battered, old suitcases from under the bed.

"Get your things together, Joe," she said. "We're going home."

We quickly packed the cases with the few belongings we had, picked them up and ran all the way to the railway station. As we ran for the train to head north, the bells of St Mary's Church were chiming.

I knew then I would not be returning to Oldham and, despite the uncertainty of what lay ahead, I was relieved to be out of the mill town, out of the unfriendly school, and on my way home.

Within half an hour my mother and I were on the train. We changed at Manchester and when we sat on the train heading for Newcastle, I cuddled up to her. After we arrived in Newcastle, we got a bus to New Kyo and didn't arrive at my grandmother's house until very late at night.

When she opened the door my grandmother's expression, and that of my Uncle Jimmy, who stood behind her, was that of elation. The adults stayed awake talking for much of the night; there was a lot to talk about, while I slipped into the familiar bed, with the paraffin lamp burning nearby.

For some reason, I thought I could faintly hear the chimes of St Mary's Church clock. But that was just in my imagination. I drifted to sleep, and it was the best night's sleep I had had for weeks.

Chapter Six

On a bright, but cold, day, I was walking to my grandmother's house in Dudley Terrace, after having bought a packet of sweets from Francis' shop on the corner, when I noticed a figure in uniform walking towards me.

Initially, as the sunlight burst through the clouds and the rays scorched the dusty terraces, I was temporarily blinded by the light.

Then, as the figure drew closer and the sky slightly clouded over, I saw the three stripes on the arms of his uniform.

He ran towards me, scooped me up into his arms and embraced me. He pushed the hair away from my brow, and I knew he was looking to see if the fractured skull I suffered all those years ago had left a permanent mark.

It was April, 1947, and I had just turned 12. It was almost seven years since I waved my father goodbye when he jumped into the Army wagon in New Kyo and headed off to war. It had been a long seven years and so much had happened.

My father, who had now attained the rank of Colour Sergeant, looked bronzed and healthy. In recent months he had been stationed at Dover, helping soldiers discharged from the Army

He carried me in his arms to my Aunt Nellie's house in the street, sat me down on a chair, and sat opposite. He told me how much he had missed me and we both started to cry. We both cried for a long time.

Other relations were in the house, my cousins Ellen and Rachel, Ralph, my Uncle Emmerson and Aunt Nellie. It was a house full of tears.

As we looked at my father, and told him how delighted we were to see him again my mother appeared at the door, looking slightly agitated.

"What's going on?" she asked.

As she entered the room, she could see that everyone was tearful and then she spotted my father, who turned to look at her, but there was no malice in his eyes. My mother's eyes filled with tears. This was the first time in many years she had been in my Aunt Nellie's house, even though they lived so close by.

As she asked my father how he was, I felt a faint hope that they might embrace. But too much had happened in the seven years they had been apart. There was some bitterness there, but it manifested itself only in the stilted conversation between them. I could tell my mother felt uncomfortable, perhaps, in the circumstances, that was unavoidable.

My father indicated he would like to see my grandmother, and my mother suggested he should come over. I walked downstairs with my mother and father and we crossed the street to 11 Woodbine Terrace. My grandmother was surprised but pleased to see my father in the house, as was my Uncle Jimmy. My father sat down and went on to ask how everyone was. It all seemed very pleasant, but beneath the surface there was obvious bitterness.

Personally, I was absolutely delighted that here I was sitting in the same room as the people I loved most; my mother, father, my grandmother and my Uncle Jimmy. Despite the obvious awkwardness, that day was one of the happiest of my life.

During the time he was in the house, he asked my mother how she was keeping, and whether she was staying with my grandmother. She replied she had been away for some time, but that was all over now, and that she was living with my grandmother and me.

The atmosphere changed in the next few minutes. My grandmother suggested my father should come over the next day for tea and that we should invite Aunt Meggie and other members of the family. A family tea? Having never expected this family meeting to take place that day, I was overwhelmed and excited at the prospect of a family tea.

After my father returned to my Aunt Nellie's house, I sat with my mother and grandmother.

"It's such a great shame, such a shame, all that has happened," my grandmother said, as she dabbed her eyes with a handkerchief.

My mother broke down and started sobbing inconsolably. She went into the next room and stayed there for a full 15 minutes. When she returned, her eyes were red and swollen.

Within our family we had a situation where my mother no longer had anyone, and lived with my grandmother and myself and my Uncle Jimmy. My Aunt Meggie's husband had left her. And only a few doors away my father was staying the night with other members of the family. It all seemed so disjointed, so dysfunctional. Most of the other families in the neighbourhood appeared to have parents with stable relationships. It was something that perplexed me for many years.

My Aunt Nellie, my father's sister, lived opposite my grandmother in Dudley Terrace. I used to speak to her two daughters, my cousins Rachel and Ellen, and her son Ralph. I didn't have a great deal to do with my Aunt Nellie or Uncle Emmerson. My mother discouraged me from associating with them, and I assumed it was because of the fall out between my mother and my father.

There was a lot of acrimony and bitterness within the family. My mother wasn't their most popular person. They would pass in the street without talking to her.

The Bevan Boy Peter, from Oldham, had put in an appearance at my grandmother's front door a few months before my father's homecoming, pleading for a reconciliation with my mother. She had resisted, though I had the sneaking suspicion she had mixed feelings about rejecting him. Peter went back to Lancashire, never to be seen again.

The eagerly-awaited family tea arrived at my grandmother's house and when my father entered, with a beaming smile on his face, my Aunt Meggie embraced him long and hard. My grandmother, my mother and I also sat around the dining table and we discussed family affairs, but there was always one subject, that of Oldham, which was not on the agenda.

My father asked me how I had been getting on with the showgroups, and I told him I had been out of it a little since the move to Oldham. I could have bitten my tongue. My mother glanced at me disapprovingly, so I moved the conversation on quickly, talking about another showgroup that I hoped to get involved with.

My father told us he had work to complete at Dover, but he would be back in New Kyo within about six months. I wondered where he would be living, with Aunt Nellie? My mother was more forthcoming about her plans, saying she was looking for a new home for her and I. I got the distinct impression the signs were being put out by my mother that she wouldn't be unhappy if some form of reconciliation was to take place.

My imagination ran riot that day. I went to bed that night with a very warm glow. I hoped and prayed my parents might get together again. I was happy enough living with the knowledge that my parents were currently at least in close proximity. My biggest desire was to see us all living together again as a family.

The following day my father came over to my grandmother's and asked my mother if she had any objections to him taking me to London for two weeks. He was seeing a cousin of his in

Fulham. I was delighted when my mother agreed. It would give my father and I a real opportunity to get to know each other after our enforced near seven-year separation.

Very early one morning two weeks later, my father and I embarked on a London-bound train at Newcastle. It was the first time I had been up when it was still dark. My father was in his uniform and was carrying his regimental case.

The journey to London took about six hours and we talked and talked. He mentioned little about Oldham but I told him I was unhappy there. I often wondered whether I had said too much.

In London, we took the underground to Fulham, a completely new experience for me, and we stayed at my father's cousin's house. His cousin and the rest of his family were very pleased to see us, and we all stayed up talking until quite late in the night.

Over the following few days we visited many sites, including Buckingham Palace and the areas bombed by the Luftwaffe. I had a great time with my father..

When I got back home to my grandmother's house in New Kyo, I talked at great length about my trip to London – and bored everyone.

A few days later, Aunt Meg and my mother and father went out for a drink in Stanley. I thought this was a great development and my imagination started running riot again. My father bought me a new bike from a shop in Stanley – bikes were in short supply after the war – and I rode it enthusiastically from Stanley to New Kyo, eager to show my friends. Things were really looking up for little Joe Mills.

About a month after my trip to London, my father took me to Pontefract to see his half-brother Will Mills, and again I met more cousins and friends and had an enjoyable time. In Pontefract, as in London, my father never left my side. I was fascinated to know I had so many cousins from my father's side of the family.

Back in New Kyo, my father started appearing more and more at grandmother's house, talking to my mother, my grandmother and Aunt Meggie. And all the while I was looking for the signs that would suggest my big wish might come true. One evening my father called on my mother and the two of them went out for a night, unaccompanied. Things, I thought, could only get better.

In the village, my cousins Ellen and Rachel who lived with Aunt Nellie told me the family gossip was that my father and mother may get together again. I asked my grandmother if there was any truth in it. "Wait and see", my grandmother told me. "Wait and see."

My father returned to Dover to finish his term of office and in New Kyo there was talk about moving house. I heard Aunt Meggie talking with my grandmother about her moving out of the house in Woodbine Terrace and back to Percy Terrace so the young couple that had moved upstairs, Bob Seymour and his wife, could move downstairs with their two young children. It didn't occur to me then that the move here and the move there was all to accommodate my mother and father getting back together again.

When my father returned from Dover on leave, I was told by both my parents that they had agreed to get married again. Their divorce had only been absolute for ten months. I was absolutely ecstatic.

The ceremony took place in the register office at Harelaw, near Catchgate. My father wore his Army blues, my mother was very smart and all the family were there. A big photograph of the wedding appeared in the local paper, the Stanley News.

Again, this was something of a first. Here I was aged 13 at my parents' wedding.

We moved into the house in New Kyo and my father spent all his discharge money on new furniture, and even a new clippy

49

mat. I was proud to invite my friends into the house, and they said it was the poshest house in the street.

At the age of 13, this was my sixth house.

One day, sitting at the table with my mother and father, enjoying a meal, the memories of my accident, my father going to war, the blue letter which I read and shouldn't have, and the painful, poverty-fuelled days in Oldham, were now all just a distant blur. I was happy at home with my family.

Chapter Seven

The miners in the pit village of New Kyo and surrounding villages worked the seams at the Morrison North pit in Annfield Plain. The pit was part of everyday life, providing work for local men, a wage at the end of the week, and the Miners' Welfare Hall, where pitmen and their families sought entertainment at weekends. For many families in New Kyo, life revolved around the pit.

So when, on a Friday in August 1947, an explosion ripped through the pit, killing 21 miners, there was a collective grief around New Kyo, Annfield Plain and surrounding villages; a grief that was almost tangible.

Some miners were known to take their cigarettes and tobacco down the pit with them, despite the risks involved, and after a build-up of firedamp, when one miner struck a match to light a cigarette, the inevitable explosion could be heard for miles around.

Nineteen miners choked to death, having inhaled lethal carbon monoxide and two collapsed with heart problems, after suffering serious burns. Three other miners were badly injured as a result of the blast.

One of the men who was killed, John Grimley, a 41-year-old stoneman, was known to me as a good friend of my father. John had been a sergeant in the Army and had not been long back from the war when he lost his life.

His daughter Maureen was a friend of mine and his wife,

who was known as Nan Grimley, was a good friend of my Aunt Meggie.

I remember going into Aunt Meggie's, seeing Nan Grimley in tears. I didn't know what to say, words just failed me. Her daughter Maureen was also in the room and, again, I just didn't have a clue what to say.

The gates of the Morrison pit were directly opposite St Aidan's Church where I was a member of the choir. There had been a choir practice scheduled for that evening.

I went down to the church as usual and saw tearful people milling around by the pit gates, anxiously waiting for news of their loved ones. When my friends and I went into the church, we were told by the choirmaster that because of the terrible accident that had happened that day the choir practice would have to be cancelled.

The after-effects of the disaster were felt around the area for many weeks. It was as if the heart had been ripped out of these communities. The explosion had been devastating, with terrible consequences for many local families.

For the next few weeks at St Aidan's Church, services were related to the mining disaster. For several weeks, the local pit villages were in mourning.

My father had been discharged from the Army at about this time. He was very upset when he heard about the death of his friend John Grimley.

He kept up his interest in the Territorial Army, taking up the position of storeman and Colour Sergeant at the TA's headquarters in Stanley.

He started work at Craghead Colliery, developing new seams and his job involved working with explosives. After several years in a PoW camp, my father was back to square one, working down the local pit.

I joined the Army Cadets and I was growing ever closer to

my father. I learned how to dismantle guns and put them back together, and by the time I was 16-and-a-half I reached the rank of Sergeant in the Cadets, something that made my father proud. With the TA, I also went to various Army camps.   Despite all this activity, my schoolwork didn't suffer, I was always in the top four or five academically.

My stage days continued and I joined a new showgroup in South Moor run by a Mrs Veal, who lived next door to my grandmother's cousin. It was different from what I had done in the past and I did a few shows but lost interest after a few months, thinking I should be doing something a little more adult, though many people tried to encourage me to stay. They thought I had a natural talent.

Several people used to come back to our house after the local workingmen's club had closed at about 10pm for supper and it was really because of my mother's meat pies. She was an extremely good cook. My father used to lend a hand by making pea and ham soups from shanks that I used to buy at Castle's the butchers.

It was a very friendly and homely atmosphere and, as a boy, I enjoyed listening in to the conversations.

At supper the discussions went on to early in the morning. It was quite interesting sitting around listening to these people talking about the war and related topics. Quite often they used to talk about the club entertainment and the turn that had been on that evening. It used to remind me that when I got a little older I could make some money in the clubs, entertaining the crowds with my song and dance routines.

Another friend who used to come over from time to time was Jackie Elliott with his wife Elsie. He was a miner but was also the barman at the club. Elsie was a terrific pianist.

She always played by ear. It amazed me how easily she could pick up tunes in this way.

I had many friends in and around New Kyo; Eric Dodds, whose nickname was Shadrack because of an interest he had in the Egyptian Pharaohs; Norman Robson who hadn't been long in New Kyo and was keen on entertainment and whose uncle led a showgroup called the Four Jones' Boys, and many others. One of the Jones' Boys, whose name was Bernie, if I remember rightly, later married a very well-known singer during the 1950s, Ruby Murray.

I remember once going to see a friend's uncle playing at the Empire in Newcastle and being invited backstage. I was gobsmacked to see in the dressing room Tommy Cooper, who was just starting his career as the mad magician. I was surprised at how tall he was.

On a Saturday, I would meet the Co-op milkman and help him with his rounds, and the few shillings I earned I would spend in Francis' corner shop.

Showgroups, entertainment, and listening to musical variety shows on the wireless, occupied much of my spare time, and my mother, as always, was keen on pushing me in that direction as much as she could.

When the voice broke of the boy who played Just William in the popular BBC radio programme my mother wrote off to the BBC and secured me an audition for the part. We went to Newcastle for the auditions and there was 12 other boys vying for the part. I was asked to read from a script for about ten minutes. Afterwards, they thanked me for my attendance but I didn't get the part.

Shortly after my first proper audition, my mother decided that I needed voice training. She had high hopes that one day my name would appear on some billboard outside a local theatre. We went through to Newcastle again, to a singing teacher in Benwell, where I had to sing the scales as the teacher sat at a very large piano. He told my mother I could attend lessons, but despite my mother's burning desire to see improvement in my singing and dancing skills, the cost of the voice training lessons was out of the reach of an ordinary mining family like ours. My mother was quite disappointed, but personally I was slightly relieved. I really couldn't see myself as a professional singer and dancer.

However, along with the rest of my friends from Annfield Plain School, I had reached the age when decisions had to be made about what I wanted to do with the rest of my life. In New Kyo there appeared to be little choice; the pit, the brickyards, Consett Ironworks. Some of my friends had already decided what they were going to do. Tommy Christer was to work in the dairies; Walter Hole and Joe Bell were destined for the local pit; Freddie Tempest was also off to the dairy, where the conditions and pay were reasonable, and Tommy Elliott decided he would hang on in for an apprenticeship.

My parents were quite emphatic that I wasn't to go down the pit or to the Consett Iron Company, which they thought was too far away. Like Tommy Elliott, they thought I should try and get some form of apprenticeship.

I did have some experience of life in the mines. When I was about 14 my father took me on a visit to Craghead Colliery and I saw the terrible conditions the miners were expected to work in. With all the dust around, and the state of the pit ponies, I really thought it wasn't a place where anyone should be expected to work.

As for an apprenticeship, I really didn't know what I was looking for. I didn't have any engineering skills and I knew nothing about motor cars. A decision, however, needed to be made soon.

My teenage years had begun with my father returning home from war, soon followed by the catastrophic event of the Morrison pit explosion. Two more sad events left their mark on my teenage years; the death of my beloved grandmother and the death soon afterwards of my Uncle Jimmy. My parents often said Jimmy died from a broken heart after the death of his sister, my grandmother. They were very close. The truth is, it was probably his diet that killed my Uncle Jimmy. He had an extremely hearty appetite and ate all the wrong type of foods for a man his size, 20 stone and only about 5ft 4ins. The loss of my grandmother and my Uncle Jimmy, who had both cared for me so much when I needed them most, left me feeling very sad.

Chapter Eight

Standing in the corner at the Co-op Dance Hall in Stanley on a Saturday night, dressed in our best clothes and listening to the modern dance music, was something we didn't really have in mind when myself and a group of friends graduated from the local picture hall and the ice cream parlour to dance nights ... and girls.

The music was good, but my nights with the showgroup at New Kyo Miners' Welfare Hall and other halls in County Durham, my time with Effie Wilson's team of dancers, and even the expert tuition from my clog-dancing Uncle Jimmy, hadn't prepared me for the modern dance scene in any way.

Being able to tap dance, even with jingling heels, was one thing for a young boy with his heart on the stage and his dream of being in the spotlight. But that wouldn't impress the pretty girls gliding around the dance floor, clinging to their partners, to the beat of the latest modern ballroom dancing tune.

I couldn't do any of these modern dances at all, and stood idly around with my friends, who were equally talentless in the modern dancing stakes, watching everyone on the dance floor appearing to have a whale of a time. We really must have looked a pitiful sight.

On the other side of the dance hall stood a number of girls, who appeared to be as ignorant as ourselves about the vagaries of the quick step or St Bernard's Waltz.

We chatted to the girls and soon realised they were in a very similar predicament to ourselves.

For a young lad such as myself, who had soaked up the applause at many halls with my tap dancing routines, and who loved music, the sight of the couples waltzing around the dance hall in Stanley, made me envious to the point of action.

Returning home one night from the dance hall, I mentioned my predicament to my father. He and my mother were both good ballroom dancers.

"There's no point going to a dance, if you can't dance," my father said. "And you really have to be able to dance, if you want a girl."

Over the next few weeks in the front room of our house in New Kyo my parents taught me how to waltz, the quick step and the St Bernard Waltz, as well as some of the other popular dances of the time. I didn't mention this to my friends because, whatever my intentions, I could envisage their taunts of "cissy" had they known.

After the expert tuition from my parents, a Saturday night dance at the Stanley Dance Hall arrived and I met up with my friends at an ice cream shop beforehand. It was a cold night and some of my friends were more keen on having a night at the picture house.

"You won't get a girl at the picture house," I told them. "They'll all be at the dance."

Shortly after we arrived in the dance hall, we stood around, as usual, eyeing up the girls and listening to the music.

The band leader announced the St Bernard's Waltz and I casually walked away from my friends, in the direction of the girls standing opposite.

"Where are you going?" One of my friends asked. "Watch, and learn," I said, more tongue-in-cheek than out of bravado.

As my friends looked on, obviously believing I was about to make a real fool of myself, I asked one of the girls if she would like to dance. My friends were astonished and burst out laughing. But when I started confidently gliding around the dance floor, with a pretty girl in my arms, they were even more amazed. After the St Bernard Waltz, came the quick step, followed by a waltz, then another quick step. At long last I was able to go to the dance, and dance, rather than stand around on the periphery of the dance floor looking out of it.

It soon dawned on my friends that I must have been having dancing lessons and when I told them I had been taking lessons from my parents, they were surprised and one or two said their fathers might play football with them, but they would draw the line at teaching them the quick step. They were unwilling to ask their parents to teach them how to dance – so I took it upon myself to be their tutor.

Over the next few weeks the small back yard at our house, with grass growing through its cracked concrete, became our dance floor. And when confusion reigned about who was taking the lead, particularly among two of my friends, Walter Hole and Freddie Tempest, and who was taking the part of the woman, the yard was filled with howls of laughter.

During the next few months we began enjoying the dances and went to two or three a week. It was there that I met my first girlfriend, a girl with the colourful sounding name of Carol Rainbow. She lived at Quaking Houses, another typical pit village a mile up the road from South Moor. Her father worked at the local colliery and she had two sisters and a brother. I would meet her at the ice cream shop or the dance hall, and see her to her bus.

Carol was a very nice girl and after a few weeks I was invited to her house for tea on a Saturday. We were together, as a teenage couple, for about 18 months.

As for the job situation, I did not end up down the pit, as my mother and father had hoped, but I also avoided the usual route of entering the employment of the local brickyards or the Consett Ironworks.

Thanks to my father, who had spoken on my behalf to the manager of Brough's grocer's store in Stanley, a Mr Thompson Cook, I started my working life in the retail business, as an apprentice grocer.

Mr Cook told me that as I had been heavily involved in showgroups throughout the area, many customers may know me, and this could work in the store's favour.

I started in Brough's in Stanley in mid-year and my first uniform wasn't a white pinny-type coat, as I expected, it was a large brown coat; too large, in fact. I had to roll up the sleeves and the coat tails trailed along the floor behind me, causing much mirth among the rest of the staff. I took the coat home and my mother altered it for me.

As an apprentice, I had to learn all aspects of the retail trade and my first job in the warehouse involved the weighing of provisions, cutting cheeses, and stocking shelves.

I worked alongside two elderly gentlemen, who had been at Brough's for many years and appeared to be a little settled in their ways, but I soon cheered them up, I thought, with a little light-hearted banter and a few witty quips. The women in the store often had a few laughs at my expense. Sometimes the banter was of an adult nature, and I would become embarrassed and uncomfortable.

"What do you expect from a New Kyo choirboy?" one of the more raucous woman workers would say.

The weekends after work, if I wasn't working in Brough's store on a Saturday morning, were the usual routine with my friends around New Kyo. We very rarely ventured out of the village.

On a Friday night, we would meet up and compare the wages we had received. Walter and Joe Bell and Alan Hands, who all worked at the pit sorting the coal from stone, always had a little more in their wage packets than I did.

On a Saturday, we would all play football on Kyo Bogs and talk about watching Newcastle United playing at St James's Park and then we'd catch Jimmy Downs, selling the Football Pink, and see how the club had fared.

Our interest in Newcastle United, at least for a year or two, never stretched to visiting the city's ground. The folklore among the people in New Kyo and Annfield Plain was that the people of Newcastle were very hard and if you did visit Newcastle you would be beaten up.

Fish Meggie, a fish wife from Tynemouth, a small woman who always wore a type of sack-cloth dress and a shawl, would knock door-to-door, selling fresh cod, kippers and other seafood for a few shillings. Then the Singing Buskers would call, usually singing religious-type songs and the next day the Salvation Army brass band would follow in their footsteps, spreading the gospel through their hymns and prayers.

I was still attending the church choir, though that petered out in the months ahead. While the women folk prepared Sunday dinner, the men of the village would be up to the workingmen's club for a session; a few pints and a game of cards or dominoes. And they'd chat about the conditions at work, the poor pay and how much coal the pit had produced that week.

The men would return home from the club with a bottle of beer and a bottle of lemonade to make shandy for the family to drink during their dinner. On his way home, my father would pick up a Sunday newspaper, then lie on top of the bed and go to sleep for a couple of hours. After his dinner, like most other men in the village, he would have a wash and shave at about 6 o'clock and then turn out for another session at the club. This was a typical weekend in New Kyo, not just for my family but for many others, who couldn't, or didn't, want to see beyond the village boundary walls.

There was a group of travelling salesmen at Brough's who worked from the shop, going out every day to Stanley and Annfield Plain to take orders from homes. The salesmen wore suits, carried a book and had a bag strapped across their shoulders. They would get their basic salary and a bonus based on the amount of sales they made. I thought this would be an interesting job but never thought I would be doing it.

The store manager Thompson Cook asked me to go to the office one morning to ask me to take over a round in the Shield Row area, as one of the salesmen had to take time off on the sick. Thompson gave me a book, containing a list of addresses, and a black bag.

A large lady opened the door at the first house I called at. I was invited in and then asked for her order. She ran through her few requirements, bacon, sugar, eggs, bread, and I tried a sales pitch, suggesting she might want to try some of other Brough's products. I secured a good order from the woman, and decided to adopt the same sales technique at every house I called at. I didn't get back to the shop until about 4pm, when the normal finishing time was about 1pm. I handed my book to Thompson Cook, who appeared a little worried. He looked at my order book, laughed out loud, and took the book away. He came back after an hour to tell me I had increased sales that morning by 25 per cent.

During the next few weeks, I covered for salesmen who were on the sick or on holiday in Annfield Plain, Shield Row, South Moor and New Kyo. The good orders I was bringing in was reflected in my pay packet at the end of the week, with a decent commission. My sales success caused some resentment among a few of the salesmen who had been with Brough's for several years.

As part of my indentures, I travelled to Rutherford College in Newcastle every Tuesday to learn about the retail trade; always looking over my shoulder in case of an attack from a Townie. I met many people in the retail trade from different shops around the region, including Newcastle, Northumberland and Yorkshire.

Things at Brough's became a little more pressurised. I felt I was trying to achieve and wasn't being encouraged. When I announced my intention to break my indentures I was surprised at how many people came to me, who had not seemed supportive in the past, urging me to stay on. My parents were not very happy about it and my father and Thompson Cook had a number of discussions. But I was determined I wanted to move on.

I got a job at the local Co-op Dairy as a roundsman and I was allocated a very large area in Whickham, Gateshead.

My mother and father became a little disillusioned with me, believing I was going nowhere with my job at the dairy. I did remind them that the tips I had made in the run-up to Christmas had enabled me to take driving lessons and I would soon have a driving test. This didn't impress my parents at all and they suggested I should find some form of apprenticeship.

I did become a little disillusioned with life shortly afterwards and felt I should look for something else. I started buying copies of The Stage magazine and looked at the adverts and had my imagination fired up when I saw ads for auditions for the shows. But I could have ended up in London with nothing.

One day while I was in the house there was a knock on the door and it was a chap named William Foster, who went to St Patrick's School in Dipton, not far from Annfield Plain, and was involved in the Irish dancing scene. He had come to ask my father for a reference to join the Army. He had already had an interview at the recruiting agency in South Shields.

He seemed very enthusiastic and my father gave him a reference. When he left the house, I turned to my parents and said I was still a member of the Army cadets, which I enjoyed, and asked if they thought the Army might suit me as a career. We discussed this at length.

Within a day or two my father took me to the recruiting centre in South Shields and I signed up for three years with the Royal Electrical and Mechanical Engineers (REME)

I was given the Queen's shilling and that was it. I would soon be saying goodbye to the streets of New Kyo, for a destination yet to be decided.

Chapter Nine

My opponent was tall, muscular, and judging by the number of badges on his trunks, he must have fought the Army's best, and possibly floored most of them. My experience in the ring had been limited to a few bouts at the Army Cadet base in Stanley, and I had to be the first to admit I was no big hitter.

As hundreds of people sat in the massive gym at the camp, looking on, and my opponent psyched me out with his frosty stare, I could only think tactics. There was no way I could have beaten this chap, and it was looking unlikely that I'd even go the distance.

"Stamp, shuffle, stamp." The commands of my old dance teacher Mrs Effie Wilson started ringing in my ears. "Stamp, shuffle, stamp."

The bell went for round one and he came at me fast and hard, but his right hand missed the target as I deftly shuffled around on the canvas, ducking, diving, bobbing, weaving, shuffling, stamping and shuffling again.

The crowd of soldiers, particularly the senior officers in the front rows, were in stitches, as I confused my opponent by dancing around the ring, avoiding virtually every punch he threw. This may have been a serious bout for my opponent, but, for me, it was showtime.

By the end of the fight, my opponent was exasperated and demoralised, he hadn't been able to make head nor tail of my tactics. When the referee took us back into the centre of the ring, and took hold of our gloves, my opponent got the decision, but I received the loudest applause. The boxer said I had made a mockery of the whole event and should be ashamed of myself. As far as I was concerned, I was unmarked , I hadn't been humiliated and I had entertained the crowds. My tactics had paid off.

When the MC presented the trophies, I was thanked for the best entertainment of the evening.

The boxing match came near the end of my training at my third Army camp, Barton Stacey in Dorset, and a few weeks before my "real" posting for the three years I would spend with REME.

My first camp was at Blandford, also in Dorset, between Salisbury and Bournemouth, and my journey to it, first the bus from New Kyo, then the seven-hour train journey from Newcastle, then the long journey from London, gave me ample time to consider whether I was doing the right thing. At the age of 17, this was my first time away from home alone and I was, naturally, apprehensive.

Spending two-and-a-half years with the Army Cadet Force, and achieving the rank of sergeant, would help me in the Army, I thought. I had passed my driving test and had some experience of working with people in the retail world, and I had driven a large milk delivery wagon, as the second man, around the streets of Whickham in Gateshead.

My cadet training, I was to learn, counted a little but the rest meant nothing as far as my Army training was concerned. I was really starting out all over again, learning the basics and having to adopt to the strict discipline and the strict routine of Army life.

When I arrived at the Blandford camp, tired and hungry after the long and tedious journey south, I met a few other raw recruits from different places across the country. We were told to put our bags into a small room and then it was off to the NAAFI canteen for a bite to eat. We were greeted by a round of sarcastic applause and whistles from the hundreds of squaddies.

The squaddies gathered around the new recruits and for the next two hours they told us the horror stories of the "hell" camp we had found ourselves in. The indoctrination was sharp and it was thorough. As I lay in one of the six beds in the billet that night – our temporary accommodation – I honestly thought I had made the biggest mistake of my life. Another recruit in a bed further up the billet had obviously really let the horror stories get to him. He cried himself to sleep.

The next morning, the demon barber attacked my head with a pair of heavy clippers, leaving me virtually bald, we were subject to a thorough medical and then shown to a larger billet which would be our home for the coming weeks. We met some of the other recruits we had seen in the NAAFI the night before and yet more horror stories unfolded about the harsh discipline and strict regimentation of the camp.

After lunch we lined up in front of the drill sergeant. He bawled out what he expected from us, and said if anyone stood out of line he would stand on a wall surrounding the camp and "piss on our heads from a great height". I laughed at this, but his menacing stare told me it wasn't a joke.

Over the next six weeks, all that was expected was realised. The equipment had to be spotlessly clean, the beds made up every morning, there were regular kit checks, square bashing, and all the other routine tasks that instilled in us raw recruits a sense of order and discipline. This was the Army I had read about in books.

I met a recruit from Walthamstow, Bert Pocket, who had also been in the cadets. We became great friends. Bert and I thought that if we were finding the pace difficult, what with our cadet training, it must have been ten times worse for the really raw recruits whose knowledge of the Army was limited to what they read in the newspapers or heard on the radio.

Apart from the moans and groans about the repetitive drills, the routine manoeuvres, the hard physical training, the regimentation, the discipline and the excessive, almost obsessive, kit cleaning, there was a real sense of camaraderie in our billet.

One of the recruits, a lad from Cumbria, was unable to march swinging his arm and his leg in opposite directions. He completely lacked any sense of co-ordination. We spent many nights marching up and down the billet, showing him how to march properly. He eventually mastered it.

In the last week of our training, we were advised by the Drill Sergeant and the Sergeant Major that they would be choosing a champion recruit from the 200 or so, based on all the training that had taken place.

Two days before our Friday passing out parade I was told by the Sergeant that Bert Pocket and I had tied for the champion recruit and the matter would be decided on the firing range the next day. That sent cold shivers down my spine as I was no good on the firing range. As expected, Bert Pocket won the day and was rewarded champion recruit and I was runner-up.

On the day of the passing out parade, with the regimental band playing, Bert and I had to come before the front of the parade, down our rifles and march up to receive our medals from the Colonel. We received our medals, marched back, fell in line, and the parade marched off. It was a very proud moment for me after six weeks at training at Blandford. Secretly, though, I had hoped to win the championship.

Prior to the passing out parade, lists were posted on the drawing board, indicating what our next camp would be. For three months I was to train as a gun fitter. I couldn't think what a trained gun fitter would do in New Kyo – unless a revolution was planned.

After the passing out parade there was a big party in the

NAAFI canteen, where everyone appeared a lot more relaxed and friendly. A lot of people did a bit of a turn and I decided to give a rendition of one of my favourite numbers, kicking myself into a dance routine. Despite my heavy uniform and big Army boots, my efforts were met with loud applause.

We all got our photographs taken which were signed by the Sergeant Major and sent out within the next two weeks. He wrote that, as far as soldiering was concerned, I wasn't a bad dancer. I took that as a compliment.

I arrived in my second camp, Bordon in Hampshire, not far from the big Army town of Aldershot, on a train known as the "Bordon Bullet". I was the only recruit posted to Bordon from Blandford, so I knew there would be a different set-up to get used to, new friends to meet and new challenges to consider.

I was allocated the last bed in a billet. Everyone else on the course had arrived before me. A group of about 30 of us turned up at the recruiting office the following day and as we lined up, the Sergeant asked who had engineering experience. Twenty nine hands shot up; the hand that remained down was mine. Boning bacon at Brough's in Stanley, of course, didn't qualify.

The Sergeant told me I would need to catch up as best as I could.

We had to strip down big Army guns and put them back together again. It all seemed pretty pointless to me.

After about four weeks we moved on to the bigger guns, mounted on tanks and other big Army vehicles, and my driving licence and the driving experience on my milk round in Whickham, came in handy. I was given the task of moving some of the big low loaders around the barracks; Scammel's and the mighty Amatars. I realised then that this was the job for me, and could help me get a job in civvie street once my training days were over.

There was little to do at Bordon Camp on the evenings,

other than sit around in the NAFFI. I couldn't get any leave from the course and was virtually stuck there for two months. Some of the recruits were able to go home to London at weekends, but there just wasn't the time for me to travel to New Kyo and back.

I wrote a lot of letters to my family at home, and to the girl with the colourful name, Carol Rainbow, but their replies just made me feel very homesick

However, there was one weekend I was invited to spend with Bobby Homans and his family at Harrow on the Hill. Bobby's brother, Ronnie, was a singer who toured the London clubs and was involved in showgroups. At one club, I did a song and dance routine which went down very well and I was asked to do one or two encores. I was able to relax and enjoy myself.

One morning over breakfast Ronnie asked me to join his showgroup and tour the clubs of London, telling me what a great opportunity it would be. It was a great idea, but I had signed up with the Army for three years. I put the whole idea to the back of my mind. It made me a lot more unsettled than I had been previously.

I left Bordon when the course had finished and took the train to Barton Stacey, the heavy transport division of REME. Again, I was confronted by a number of squaddies who felt duty bound to tell me the horror stories of their stay at the camp. The discipline was such that two recruits had jumped over the wall and were wanted for desertion.

With so much heavy transport, the camp was under strict security, always on the alert for terrorist attacks, ringed by high security fences. It was more like a prison camp than Blandford or Bordon, but when I thought about what my father had to endure as a Prisoner of War, things were really put into perspective.

When I arrived with a few others, we were shown into a

billet and met one or two soldiers who had been there for a number of weeks. Again, they had tales of horror to relate to the newly-arrived recruits. The stories, like the stories I had heard previously, were so familiar. There appeared to be a pattern, repeated at all the camps at the start of any fresh, new, intake.

Each recruit was given an instructor for a month, mine was a corporal from Liverpool. He told me he aimed to make my life hell, to make sure I got through the driving tests, not knowing I already had a full driving licence. When I told him this, he was ecstatic, and said the next four weeks would be more like a holiday.

I didn't realise what he meant until we left the camp and drove around the countryside. For the next four weeks I had to get used to driving the big Army trucks and wagons, but often we would park up in the countryside, put the handbrake on, relax, and talk. And when it came to me taking the various tests, the corporal was happy for senior officers to believe he had trained me up to the required standard.

About five or six weeks into the course I was asked if I wanted to stay on as a driving instructor. I turned down the offer, preferring to stay on driving the big and often heavily- armoured trucks that required more than a little skill to be able to manoeuvre properly.

One day, a welcome diversion from the old routine arrived when I, along with three or four other recruits, was asked to clean up a very large room in the camp, which was strewn with maps, different coloured ribbons, and miniature model vehicles and other equipment. We were promised we could get off early the following day if we did a reasonable job, so we set about cleaning the room with gusto, tipping everything into bins and boxes. After a couple of hours the room looked immaculate.

The Welsh Sergeant, who had given us the orders, returned to the room, stood at the door, and almost fainted. What my colleagues and I had managed to achieve in two hours was to destroy weeks of strategic thinking by very high ranking officers at the camp who had drawn up detailed plans for regimental manoeuvres, code-named Operation Gold Flash

The visibly shaken Welsh Sergeant, understandably bawled us out of the room and the next day we had to appear before the Colonel. We were given a dressing down, which was what we expected. The Welsh Sergeant, however, was never seen on camp again, much to the delight of scores of squaddies who burst into applause when my colleagues arrived at the NAAFI that night. It never ceased to amaze me how quickly gossip would spread around an Army camp.

A few days later regimental week was upon us, which meant a lot of activity and a call for volunteers. An incentive for volunteers was a few extra days' leave at the end of the course, so I put myself forward for the boxing tournament, a football competition, and I also threw my hat in the ring for a planned variety show. The boxing bout, as I've already outlined, was more of a stage show but I was also given the opportunity to show off my singing and dancing talents at the real variety show. I was paired with another song and dance man, who had in the past appeared in shows in the West End, and we re-hearsed hard for the show.

On the night, when I entered the dressing room, I was as-tounded to see the effort that had gone in to the costumes. Clearly, people were taking the show very seriously. The stage had been magnificently designed, there was bunting all around the room, and there was a four-piece band to accompany the performers.

My colleague and I did an old-fashioned vaudeville routine, which went down very well with the audience, and with the Colonel. At the end of the show he asked me whether I had ever con-sidered entering showbusiness professionally, rather than staying in the Army.

Ever since my early days in New Kyo, I had impressed audiences with my song and dance routines, but I never thought I would get the breaks if I entered showbusiness professionally. It seemed such a precarious way to make a living; hardly any very regular work, living on your wits and with little or no security.

I was destined to perform, I thought, but mine would be a very different stage to those found in theatres or in Army training camps.

I left Barton Stacey for my extra days' leave and took the train to Newcastle and the bus to New Kyo.

It was dusk when I arrived in the village and some miners were waiting at the bus stop to get to their shift down the pit. Barking dogs ran up and down the streets, the chimneys were smoking, piles of coal stood in back lanes and the air was thick with coal dust and the stench from the outside netties.

The economic gloom and the polluted atmosphere of socially-deprived New Kyo, I knew, could be replicated in any one of the hundreds of pit communities in the North East of England. And this was a way of life people chose not to question, either because they reluctantly accepted that that was the way it was, or they had never had the opportunity to broaden their horizons to see how others lived.

I stood for a few minutes at the top of the street, put my kit bag over my shoulder, and looked around me. For the first time in my life I didn't know whether I was happy to be back home.

At number 11 Woodbine Terrace, my mother and father were delighted to see me. Aunt Meggie and some of the other members of the family planned to come round for tea the following afternoon; my mother was baking pies.

I went with my father to the New Kyo Central Club and met up with a few of my old friends, who were still working at the pits, or the brickyards or the Consett Ironworks.

And that girl with the colourful name, Carol Rainbow, I was told, was seeing someone else.

The cosy familiarity of home, the comforting sight of my mother and father, Aunt Meggie, and the rest of the family, were things I had harkened for during my homesick days in the Army billets.

But today I was asking myself, did I really want to spend the rest of my days in New Kyo?

Chapter Ten

The bricks and stones outside the guard room at Combermere Barracks in Windsor were painted white. The barracks was home to The Blues and Royals, an amalgamation of the Royal Horse Guards and the Life Guards, the senior regiment of the British Army. Inside the barracks, the equipment shone like mirrors and you could see your reflection in the guards' highly-polished black boots.

The train had pulled into Windsor in the late afternoon and from the window I could see the imposing backdrop of Windsor Castle. The whole area was lush with greenery; the buildings oozed architectural splendour; the beautiful River Thames ran alongside the railway station and nearby stood Eton College, a seat of learning for the landed gentry, where students wore Dickensian-style uniforms, spoke the Queen's English and walked so very tall. I had seen such images before, on picture postcards, but the reality was far more impressive.

Here I was in Royal Windsor, for what my father called my "real" Army posting, and these first impressions counted for a lot.

I had been met at the railway station by Jimmy, a lad from Lancashire, who was wearing dirty oil-stained overalls, a cap that appeared to have been thrown on to his head, an open-necked shirt, and who had a cigarette dangling from his bottom lip.

"Is your name Mills? he asked, as I wondered why he had been allowed out of the barracks in such a state. I climbed aboard the lorry and Jimmy, who was a welder, said he would take me on a trip around Windsor before heading for the barracks, where I was to be stationed with the Royal Electrical Mechanical Engineers (REME) as part of the Light Aid Detachment (LAD).

Jimmy told me he had been in Windsor for two years, and it had been his best posting so far. He was a regular soldier, who had signed up for nine years. He said the atmosphere at the barracks was quite relaxed and there was a lot of activity in Windsor at night, but little cash for the soldiers in our barracks to spend, as the pay was pretty poor.

As he drove around Windsor, I noticed immediately how busy and crowded the streets were. The streets were lined with many quaint and traditional-looking pubs and hotels where commissionaires, with their top hats and gleaming uniforms, stood to attention, ready to greet guests. There seemed to be a great deal happening; the streets were teeming with life and colour.

There was many coaches parked up and Jimmy told me they would have brought wealthy American tourists or other visitors from London and elsewhere into the town.

It was obvious the town was steeped in a rich history with links, through Windsor Castle, Eton, The Life Guards and The Blues and Royals, to the Royal Household.

Jimmy told me as we were driving into the barracks and down to the LAD compound that all of the captains and lieutenants within the Horse Guards were from the landed gentry; related to lords, honourables or other titled people.

As we drove into the compound I noticed a lot of horses were being led around by guardsmen dressed in their ordinary Army kit. Some were grooming the horses outside the stables. Jimmy told me this was the training area for the Household Cavalry.

The more I saw of Windsor the more I wondered how we as REME types would fit in. When we reached the end of the road in the compound, where I saw the odd armoured vehicle, it became more apparent that there was a squadron dealing with vehicle repairs. It was a funny mixture.

There was an establishment of about 30 people with the LAD and we had a captain we referred to as EME (Electrical Mechanical Engineer), a sergeant major, a sergeant and a corporal. I detected the whole area was relaxed and the discipline not as rigid as that I had come across in Blandford, Bordon and Barton Stacey.

I was told the job at the LAD was to drive the Army squadron vehicles when required to and from London's central workshops whenever they needed repair. Other than that, there wasn't a great deal more to do, other than service staff cars, but this wasn't regular work.

When I was introduced to EME, the captain, I found him to be a very relaxed individual. He was a Welshman born in Cardiff, with the surname of Smith. He told me I was the first Geordie he had had in the LADF and looked forward to working with me. I met the sergeant major, the sergeant and corporals and they were all courteous and friendly. This was quite a contrast to my previous postings.

After my evening meal, I decided to get ready in civvies and have a look around Windsor. This was quite an eye-opening experience. I noticed all the tourists with their cameras around their necks, and the scholars from Eton. At the top of the street, the entrance to Windsor Castle was guarded by the Coldstreams or the Grenadiers.

I then turned left and went past a very large hotel with commissionaires standing outside and Rolls Royce cars parked in the street. I then wandered into one of the pubs, the Star and Garter, which became very famous years later when the boxer Sugar Ray

Robinson trained there before defending his title against Randolph Turpin.

The customers in the pub were mainly the regulars and when I ordered a drink one of them picked out my accent straight away.

"A Geordie, boy. What are you doing in the area?" He asked.

"I've been transferred to Combermere for a two-year posting," I replied.

"That's not a posting," he said. "That's more like a holiday camp."

A couple of the other customers remarked on my size – 5ft 7ins – which created some laughter in the bar. That didn't worry me, it was all light-hearted and jovial. I made the Star and Garter one of my regular pubs during my time at Windsor.

Many things struck me as I walked around Windsor; the beautiful buildings, the obvious wealth of many of the residents and visiting tourists and the high levels of employment. The next day, I had a further look around the area and went to sit on the bank of the River Thames. Men in blazers with straw hats were pushing punts along the river, while scholars from Eton picnicked on the grassed areas of the river bank. When I walked back to the barracks, I did a little window shopping and noted the price of goods. Never had I seen such expensive items on sale.

The weeks and months at Windsor were very relaxed and enjoyable. Within Windsor itself, little was happening, and Jimmy's warning that I would have little cash to spend on nights out proved to be true. From the barracks, I was taking regular trips to Mill Hill in London, the REME's mechanical and maintenance depot, and on my way there and back I would make regular detours to see the sights around the capital and the surrounding countryside; cutting through the Windsor Great Park or parking up, walking into the centre and watching the Changing of the Guard.

I could understand why many young people wanted to join

the Household Cavalry. Of course height was a requirement – about 5ft 10ins. But once they got into the guards, the constant parades and spit and polish, marches, the strict discipline, and parading with the regimental bands as part of their training, caused some great stress and many of the young squaddies broke down with mental illness or sought a transfer to the armoured squadron rather than stay with the mounted squadron. I observed what was going on from close range and I could see the problems this was causing many of the soldiers.

There was another barracks in Windsor, Victoria Barracks, home to the Coldstream and the Grenadier Guards, which were equally as disciplined. I only visited Victoria barracks twice to look at problems associated with an armoured vehicle.

The rivalry between the foot soldiers of the Coldstream, The Grenadier Guards and the Household Cavalry was interesting to watch and manifested itself in fiercely competitive football matches.

All of the Guards looked very smart standing around Windsor and the tourists often stopped to take pictures. It was the expected thing for many scholars who left Eton to join the Guards, to become officers.

I often wondered how they kept to their high quality dress standards, but soon learned they all had their own batman who would press their clothes, polish their boots and polish the buttons on their tunics, and clean their quarters.

These batmen were young squaddies also doing their training and many expressed the view to me the officers used to make life hell for them, referring to them as their "fags".

The REME soldiers, on the other hand, were always treated fairly well by the Guards and other officers as they knew they would require our services from time to time, servicing their top of the range cars. Few officers had any mechanical knowledge.

Virtually all of the officers had souped-up, high performance, very expensive cars, which had to be maintained properly, and this was where the REME boys came in. Although this was technically against the rules, everyone would turn a blind eye.

I soon became a member of the servicing team and was able to earn a few pounds, which helped me enjoy the most of Windsor. I started to visit a local pub over the bridge at Eton with a Welsh colleague of mine called Taffy Waters. He was about the same height as me. We got the nicknames tweedle dum and tweedle dee among some of the Guards in the barracks because of our similar height and the fact that they thought our accents were the same.

The pub in Eton was frequented by some of the masters from Eton College and some of the senior scholars. It was a rather odd atmosphere, as there were few Army squaddie types who visited the pub other than Taffy and myself. It was an olde worlde type pub and I was fascinated by it. Taffy and I got into some very interesting debates with the Eton types. I would remark how they were all members of a privileged and wealthy elite perpetuating the problems of the deep social divisions within our country. They vigorously defended their positions and tended to look down their noses at Taffy and I.

The pub became very popular over the next few months with more and more of the scholars and their masters coming in for a pint and a debate with myself and Taffy. They called us "lefties" and claimed we wanted to start a revolution.

The landlord was a Londoner and he would slip us the occasional free drink if we could manage to keep the debates going. The Eton scholars, in their typically condescending manner, would tell us we were only mining types from up North who did not have a real grasp on the issues facing society.

Always one for a customer-boosting opportunity, the shrewd landlord decided to open up an upstairs room every Friday at about 7pm, to put the debates on a more formalised footing, even setting the agenda himself and putting a notice at the back of the bar to publicise the events. Subjects were varied, ranging from capital punishment, to privilege, the Royal family, even boating.

I regularly attended these debates on a Friday. Unfortunately, there were very few people attending from the local community. It seemed as if it was them – the Eton masters and scholars and several business people – versus us; Taffy and myself. Whatever the topic for debate, it always got around to privilege and wealth. The message we got very strongly was that people such as Taffy and myself were not really that important to society and that it was the people at Eton and other elite such places in the South who were the most important ingredient to making Britain strong.

We reacted in a typically forceful fashion, which made the debates very heated, but always good natured. One of the telling things for me about the pub was how the landlord would refer to us as Joe and Taffy, but the supercilious scholars and their masters called us simply "Mills and Waters". Perhaps they wanted to keep us in our place and avoid any misplaced familiarity.

While at Windsor, I always fancied having a picture of myself on the back of one of the Horse Guard's horses, dressed in all the guard's regalia, and I convinced one of my colleagues to allow me to do so one Saturday afternoon. I went round to the stables, got dressed with the breast plate, the hat and very large boots, and sat on a horse. As I was about to have my photograph taken one of the sergeants from the Horse Guards emerged from around the corner and asked what the **** was a grease monkey doing on the back of the horse. I jumped off the horse very quickly, the breast plate came under my chin and my hat slipped over my eyes. Fortunately, the photo was never taken, but it would have made a good one.

Another one of the activities I got involved in at Windsor was driving the officers to various functions. A lot of the officers attended the hunt and charity balls and, as copious amounts of liquor would flow at the functions, they did not wish to drive their own cars. Again, this was where the REME boys came in useful. I became one of the weekend driving team, and got to drive some very expensive motor cars around some very attractive country-side

A lot of the events were in stately homes and mansions around the area. Berkshire was very popular. The officers expected us to pick up their girlfriends, too, and take them to the events. Sometimes the wives or girlfriends would be very tipsy when they came out. Unfortunately, one of the drawbacks to this was that some of the events were quite a distance from the barracks, so we would have to wait until the function was over to bring them back.

While the officers and their wives partied upstairs, down-stairs in the servants' quarters, the cook or the maid or the butler would invite me inside for tea and sandwiches.

A few weeks before I left Windsor, we heard the REME were expected to be the support team for the Royal Tattoo to be held in Windsor Great Park behind the castle. I wasn't sure what the Tattoo was all about, but was told it was an opportunity for all the Guards in all their finery to demonstrate their horse riding and other skills in front of a large audience. REME had to ensure the proper lighting and generators were in place to make it a success.

I enquired if REME could do anything at this event. No one had any clues. We had a discussion with the Captain of the Light Aid Detachment and decided we would put an idea before the Horse Guards' committee.

As the Light Aid Detachment was a recovery unit, we devised a demonstration that would show off our skills in a positive, but humorous, way.

On the big night, about 6,000 people sat in the massive arena at Windsor Great Park and the atmosphere was electric. The band struck up and The Horse Guards and Coldstream Guards marched into the arena with all the colour and spectacle you would expect at a Royal Tattoo. The Horse Guards displayed their horsemanship with daring stunts and precision cross-over racing and gallops and the Royal Signals motorcycle display team demonstrated exactly why they are the best in the world.

Then, just before a few minutes' interval, a motorcycle from the Light Aid Detachment, with a huge metal frame surrounding it, giving it the look of Bodaecia's Chariot, swung into the showground to the tune of The Old Grey Horse Ain't What she Used To Be. The arena exploded into howls of laughter. The chariot made its way around the arena and then, suddenly, there was a huge explosion underneath the chariot and a colourful plume of smoke billowed into the air.

The driver of the chariot, Jimmy, from Lancashire, looked a bit bemused, as planned, and I, as we had rehearsed it, played the part of a Guardsman looking to see what the problem was. We gave out a big whistle and a big Army REME Scammell came into the centre of the arena and was hooked up to the chariot to "recover" it.

I looked around and saw these 6,000 people laughing and applauding and I thought this was the biggest audience I had ever been in front of. I don't know what possessed me, but I jumped on to the back of the Scammell and did an impromptu soft shoe shuffle dance to the tune that was being played by the Horse Guards Band. The driver of the Scammell didn't know what was going on and didn't want to drive the Scammell off the arena with me on top.

The whole event lasted more than 15 minutes – well over our scheduled five – and I got the distinct impression when we came off that the Horse Guards captains and other officers were not too impressed that we had overstayed our welcome.

Captain Smith, the REME captain, came over and burst out laughing. He said we had actually stolen the show. I'm not too sure if that was the case but it was a great and enjoyable event.

A few weeks later, I left Windsor having completed my three

years' service with many fond memories. I had enjoyed my time immensely with the REME attached to the Royal Horse Guards and the Life Guards.

But Windsor also left me with an impression bigger and more lasting than anything I had experienced elsewhere and formed a world view within me that I would carry for the rest of my life; a world view that would shape my thinking in so many ways.

The view was that of the gaping chasm that was the class divide; the influence and power vested in the landed gentry, who were born into wealth and who fervently believed they could justify the unfairness of the system by repeating the elitist philosophies their privilege had allowed them to acquire in the hallowed, panelled, halls of Eton and other such places.

Then there was the other divide, just as wide, between the socially and economically deprived North of England and the prosperous, affluent, so-very-different South.

Nowhere was the divides more obvious, the contrasts so stark, as in my home village of New Kyo. I hoped and prayed that one day I might be able to do something about it.

For me, Windsor was an awakening. For the first time in my life I realised that within my 5ft 7ins Northern frame beat the strong, healthy, heart of a political animal.

Chapter Eleven

I was awakened by a tap on the door at one o'clock in the morning and my father ushered me downstairs. In the living room I wiped the sleep out of my eyes and saw one the world's most famous singers sitting in an armchair by the fire. It was David Whitfield, who was then as big as Tom Jones in his heyday, and I couldn't believe what I was seeing.

That Saturday morning I had been working on my father's car, a little run-about. My father had taken a bus into Durham to do some shopping. I didn't get round to finishing the job because I couldn't find the right part and told everyone in the house when my father returned he should not move the car.

I returned from Coxhoe, where I had gone to see if I could find the right part, and saw that the car had gone, along with my father, who had decided to drive from Bowburn, where we then lived, to New Kyo to visit relatives, including Aunt Meggie. At the time I was quite worried because I hadn't fixed the problem on the car and thought my father wouldn't make it back to Bowburn.

When he knocked on the bedroom door at 1am, I thought it was to tell me he had arrived back safely. But no, he wanted to introduce me to David Whitfield, who was doing a summer season at the Theatre Royal in Newcastle at the time. My father had driven to New Kyo, as I had been told, but on the return journey, predictably, the car had broken down at Shincliffe. My father had opened up the bonnet to try to identify the problem when a big, powder blue Lincoln pulled alongside him.

"Do you need a hand?" The stranger asked, and after Mr Whitfield gave the car the once over, he pulled a towing rope from the boot of the Lincoln and towed the car, with my father and mother in the front seats, all of the two miles to Bowburn.

My father did not realise for the first five minutes just who Mr Whitfield was. When they got to Bowburn, he invited him into the house for a cup of tea.

It's not every day you find one of the world's most famous singers, sitting in an armchair in your own front room in the early hours of the morning. I spent a good hour talking to Mr Whitfield, about all the stars he had met, the places he had visited, such as Las Vegas, and, afterwards, he offered us some free tickets to see his performance in Newcastle, which we gladly accepted.

When he left, I went back to bed and reflected on this man who had image, money and influence. It had been a wonderful, unique, experience, but it proved to be a very tall tale when father and I popped into the local club for a drink the next day.

I stood at the bar with my father, who was a very honest and straightforward man, and never one to boast, and he bought his usual lottery tickets. People asked him how he was, and how the car was, knowing it had been giving him a few problems of late, and my father dropped the story into the conversation about the interesting day he had the day before when David Whitfield used his Lincoln to tow my father's car from Shincliffe to Bowburn. People stood around open-mouthed in disbelief. I tried my best to convince them the story was true, but many just thought my father had been pulling their legs.

The following week we were contacted by the News of the World, which ran a weekly column called Knights of the Road, which was to feature the story that Sunday, nominating Mr David

Whitfield as the Good Samaritan or "Knight", who assisted Durham miner Larry Mills. My father and I couldn't wait to go to the club that day, to see the faces of the disbelievers. The night before we had visited the Theatre Royal, with the complimentary tickets given to us by Mr Whitfield, and were given the best seats in the house.

A lot had happened since my days in Windsor. While I was still serving my time with the REME, my father had managed to secure a job as the manager of a pig farm in Coxhoe, County Durham, thanks to Sir Thomas Bradford, a high-ranking officer in the Territorial Army, who was also a director of Raisby's Quarry in Coxhoe. My father's TA connections helped him secure the job and he and my mother moved into a five-bedroomed house, attached to the farm, which went with the job.

However, just before I left Windsor, my parents told me that the company had decided to close the pig farm because of a lack of demand for British pork and bacon. The Danish Bacon Company had taken over many of the British markets. With my father losing his job, he lost the house that went with it, too, and had to apply to the local council for accommodation because, technically, he was homeless. He was given a small council bungalow in Bowburn. Fortunately, he was able to get a job within a few weeks at the colliery at Bowburn doing special work he had previously done at Craghead Colliery.

When I left the Army, and moved back with my parents at Bowburn, I did not expect to have great difficulties finding a job. I thought that with three years experience with the Army under my belt, and, at the age of 21 with a background in semi-skilled engineering, I would walk into a job. No one wanted gun fitters in and around County Durham.

One of the problems with living in Bowburn, five miles from Durham City, was that it wasn't close to any engineering or shipbuilding industries. The nearest heavy industry, apart from deep coal mining, was in Newton Aycliffe and Darlington.

Several times I had discussions with my father about the stark contrasts between Windsor and the poverty-stricken North East, which had the highest levels of unemployment in Great Britain, and told him how unfair it all seemed. He said it had always been the same; nothing had changed since the 1920s.

After a few weeks, I managed to find work at a local building company. Then I found a better job as a lorry driver with Dent's in Spennymoor., distributing goods in the North of England in an area stretching from Berwick down to Darlington. Eventually I started driving long distance for Dent's, seeing a lot more of the country on my travels, and always thinking how prosperous most other areas seemed when compared to the North East towns and pit villages I knew so well.

While my parents lived in Bowburn they still had lots of friends in New Kyo, and took every opportunity to visit at weekends and stay at Aunt Meggie's house. I went with them several times to see concerts and shows at the New Kyo Central Club. One of the turns one weekend was a showgroup from Newcastle called The Five Kings and Queen.

The group was very popular and my father and I went to the club early to ensure we and our company got seats. There was a large crowd and they weren't disappointed; it was one of the best shows I had seen for some time.

The main singer in the group was a girl called Shirley, who was a first-rate entertainer. At the interval I introduced myself to her and I told her about my involvement in showgroups in the past. We had an interesting chat and at the end of the night I asked her whether the Five Kings and Queen would be playing again in the area soon. She said they were in The Monkey Club, on the border of Annfield Plain, in four weeks' time, so I decided I would go and see the group again. After the show I again had a further discussion with Shirley and she told me of the other clubs the group would be playing in the area over the coming weeks. I was still very much gripped by the singing-and-dancing bug I had been bitten by at the age of about five, and I hoped the Five Kings and Queen might find room for me. My opportunity came at a club in Newcastle when one of the singers went down with a sore throat. I eagerly told the rest of the group I could stand in, and I was quite surprised when they agreed. I was reasonably happy with my performance.

Over the next few months I started seeing Shirley quite regularly, at the clubs and away from them. Eventually, I asked her if she would come down to Bowburn to see my folks. We developed a relationship from there and we decided we should get married. Her mother and father who lived in Newcastle were not very happy. They wanted her to go on the stage and didn't think she should have become involved with a long-distance lorry driver. We had a number of discussions about this. Initially, they weren't prepared to agree to the marriage, but eventually decided they would not stand in our way.

We were married in Bowburn Parish Church in April 1956, nearly two years after I left the Army in 1954. Her parents reluctantly attended the wedding, which we had to pay for ourselves, and Shirley's sister Betty was chief bridesmaid. We had a small reception in my parents' house afterwards for the family and a bigger event in the Hare and Greyhounds Pub in the evening. Our honeymoon was one night in The Royal County Hotel in Durham. That's all we could afford.

We started our married life living with my mother and father in their council house, 39 Mary Terrace, Bowburn. It was far from an ideal arrangement but we didn't have any savings to do anything else. I continued driving and Shirley got a job as a secretary with a small textile firm called Bickleys in Durham.

Two months before the birth of our first child tensions started building up between my mother and us. She constantly interfered in our affairs, even if it was with the best of intentions.

On the 17th June, 1957, our son Adrian Joseph was born at Bishop Auckland General Hospital. He had a mass of black hair and was a beautiful baby. We took him back to our home in Bowburn to share our room.

Owing to the continued tension in the house, I was encouraged to leave long-distance driving, which involved working all kinds of hours. I managed to get a local driving job with Dent's.

At about the same time, my mother had to give up work because of an injury to her shoulder. My father was still working shifts at Bowburn Colliery. The house was cramped and with a new baby crying a lot of the time, my mother's interfering ways, and much more besides, there was a great deal of tension building up in the house.

Then Shirley and I learned our second child was on the way.

My employer, Dent's, had to pay off a few drivers and put others on short-time work, which included me, so I found myself having to look for work again. A not-long married father-of-one, with another child on the way, living with my parents in a cramped, tension-filled house in the County Durham village of Bowburn. Things were going from bad to worse and I was very worried about the future.

At the age of 15, when I left school, my mother and father were adamant I should not work down the pit. Here I was now, aged 21, with new responsibilities and my options had narrowed considerably.

Bowburn Colliery was just opposite the house in Mary Terrace. Many of the local neighbours worked there. One day, inevitably, my father suggested I try to get a temporary job in the colliery "until things got better".

Working down the pit, to me, seemed the ultimate step backwards. There was further lay-offs from Dent's, and I was among them, so I was left with Hobson's Choice; work down the pit, or don't work at all.

I joined Bowburn Colliery, shunting the railway wagons into the coal filling plants so they could be filled and the coal transported to power stations throughout the country. It was hard, dirty, dusty work.

Some weeks later, I started training as a conveyor fitter, which meant better money, moving the conveyors up to the coal face, and establishing a route to ensure the coal got from the face to the top of the colliery and out for distribution.

I was working in the bowels of the earth and I experienced a comradeship and a friendship with the passionately loyal miners that I never experienced anywhere, anytime. Their spirit and humour in the face of adversity, daily risk and danger, helped me to understand in later life the reasons for their solidarity and their determination to improve conditions for their way of work and their way of life.

After my first shift doing the job I had avoided doing for the past six years, I showered and dressed. On that first day I looked in the mirror while combing my hair and saw the coal dust around my eyes. A mood of despair descended upon me and my black-ringed eyes filled with tears.

I had debated with Eton masters and scholars, beat off the competition to become runner-up in the Army's best new recruit contest. I had driven thousands of miles around the country to see how well other people lived and I had brought smiles to hundreds of faces in my younger days on stage at the Miners' Welfare Hall in New Kyo.

When I was a boy, my father worked down the pit. He still worked down the pit.

Twenty years earlier I had been in the small house in New

Kyo chatting to my mother about my father's work in the mine. And here I stood today reflecting on two men – myself and my father – over two decades.

And there was only one thing that separated us; I did not leave a black square of coal dust on my back.

That mining tradition had died and, thanks to the National Union of Mineworkers, all the collieries now had pit head baths.

Twenty years on, and the loss of the black coal dust square was the only thing that appeared to symbolise progress.

What progress?

Chapter Twelve

A small open fire stood in one corner of the squalid room at the house in Langley Moor, Durham; the house Shirley and I and our two sons, Aidan and Barry – our second son born in October, 1958 – were attempting to turn into a home.

Barry was born in Aunt Meggie's house, who had by then moved to Stanley, and the bonny lad with bright red hair joined his mother and I and his older brother at my parents' home in Bowburn.

If things were looking bleak before Barry's birth, due to the cramped conditions in the house and my mother's constant interference, after his birth things steadily worsened to the point that our marriage suffered and Shirley decided to spend more time at her parents' house in Newcastle.

The rooms at the house in Langley Moor were rented to us by a miner who worked with me in the shunting yard at Bowburn. We had to share cooking and bathroom facilities with others who lived in the house. The house, and the tension building up, often drove Shirley to despair.

I reminded her of what her parents had said when we first met; that she should have pursued a career in showbusiness. Knowing what a talented entertainer Shirley was, I did feel that I was letting her down.

My personal belief that I had failed to provide my young family with a decent first home was reinforced when Shirley's mother and father, Len and May Rusby, came to visit us at the house in Langley Moor. They both commented about the squalor in which we were living and how unsuitable it was for two very young children. They were right.

The result of discussions between Shirley and her parents on her frequent visits to Newcastle then became apparent. It seemed the three of them had drawn up a kind of masterplan which would involve me getting a new job and the four of us moving to a better house in Newcastle.

Len Rusby worked on the buses in Newcastle and his wife was a part-time barmaid at a pub in the city called the Duke of Wellington. The pub was often frequented by senior managers from the William Younger's Brewery and May often spoke to them.

She had asked one of the managers if they could offer me, her son-in-law, a job on the brewery's transport fleet as a driver and he suggested I should go in for an interview. May also told me that she had obtained the keys to a nice upstairs flat near where she lived and that we should consider renting it.

I had made a number of bad decisions in the past and did not want to make another one. There was more than myself to consider, with a wife and two young sons to look after. I agreed to the move and got a job at William Younger's Brewery and rented a reasonable flat above a greengrocer's shop in Benwell.

Hundreds of heavy barrels and crates of bottled beer were distributed every day from the brewery in Newcastle's Claremont Road to pubs and clubs throughout the North East of England.

When I started the job, a number of draymen began ribbing me about my size, 5ft 7ins and nine to ten stone, and one of them said I looked nothing like a drayman and another suggested I wouldn't last a week. It was all said in jest, and I didn't take offence. The work, though, was very heavy.

I was allocated to an articulated lorry and the driver, a man called Jimmy, was pleased to discover I had a full driving licence and had driven heavy transport for a living, both on civvie street and in the Army. As the third man on the wagon didn't drive, Jimmy knew he could have a break from the wheel, with me taking over the driving.

Just south of Newcastle, at Birtley, there was a cafe with a huge car park where many of the draymen stopped off every morning for bacon and egg sandwiches and tea before moving on with their loads to their destinations. It seemed every brewery wagon from Newcastle stopped there at about the same time. Virtually every day the drivers and draymen would chat about wages and the terms and conditions of their employment.

The rates of pay weren't too bad, but there was different rates of pay at each brewery, and this was something the poorer paid drivers and draymen were bitter about. They would also talk about the brewery owners, who appeared to be raking in millions, and the rich shareholders, who were getting richer by the day.

"All the companies are making vast profits," I said one morning, wondering how my comment would be met, as I had only just started the job. The men appeared to be listening.

"That's how the owners can send their children to the best private schools down South," I added. "Then they come back here after having had the benefits of a private education, and take over their father's brewery."

I had their attention.

"All the big brewers own large estates in Northumberland, County Durham and elsewhere," I continued. "But they've never had to get their hands dirty. The brewery owners were born into wealth. Their children are born into wealth. And so it goes on. Money, goes to money, goes to money. And for the workers who make their money, nothing improves."

I could see the drivers and draymen were agitated, thinking about their companies' profits and their own terms and conditions of employment. I had said enough. The point had been made.

At Younger's Brewery there was a small bar-type area within the workplace where workers could get a free pint after work, but it wasn't the best quality beer and staff preferred to meet up at a pub called The North Terrace for a pint and a chat. There was a lot of moans and groans in the pub after work, about how no outdoor clothing was provided for drivers and draymen during the bad weather and them having to buy their own protective clothing; the long hours which meant early starts and often late finishes; the ropes that secured the netting on the lorries being damp and dangerous. There was a lot said, but no one appeared prepared to do anything about it.

As the new kid on the block, I had to be careful what I said. Whatever was discussed at the North Terrace always found its way back to the management the next day.

During these after-work chats, I was told that the union representative had never taken up with management any of the concerns expressed. He collected contributions from the few workers who were in the Transport and General Workers' Union (T&GWU) took his 15 per cent commission, and that, it appeared, was that.

Staff who worked inside the brewery had no extras going for them, other than overtime at Christmas and other holidays.

One of the peculiar things about the conditions for the draymen, which puzzled me, was the drayman's allowance. When beer was delivered, the pub or club manager would sign for the delivery and the driver and the draymen would each be given a pint of beer or ten cigarettes, whichever they preferred. Those who didn't drink during the day took the cigarettes and could amass quite a few hundred by the end of the week, which they could smoke themselves or sell on.

Although this was called the drayman's allowance, not every manager gave them the pint or the cigarettes. I was told that the manager could account for this in his returns to the brewery, so those who didn't pay up were keeping the equivalent amount of money. This caused a lot of concern among the draymen.

Another thing I learned was that the minimum terms of conditions of employment in the breweries around Newcastle and Durham were set by a cartel, known as the Northumberland and Durham Brewers' Association. This was the brewers meeting together once a year to agree the pay rises for drivers, draymen and internal workers.

When I left the colliery at Bowburn, before moving to Newcastle, my father made sure I took my NUM card with me and told me to transfer it when I arrived at the brewery. When I gave my card to the Younger's Brewery union rep, he seemed a bit puzzled. He probably never effected a union transfer before. It took a number of weeks before I got my card back. There was an arrangement between the NUM and T&GWU whereby any previous affiliation with a union would be credited. The membership I had with the NUM was continued with the T&GWU (or the T&G, to give it its shortened abbreviation).

The Younger's brewery union rep would collect the union money on a Friday morning at the clocking-in point. He was always there with his cash bag, registering the payments in his book.

One Friday morning when we were standing around the clock, a number of people commented about the union rep being missing. It turned out he had run away with a woman from the bottling hall, and had left his wife and family.

The discussions within The North Terrace bar that evening were all about the disappearing union rep. Very little was said about finding a union replacement. I looked around at all these middle-aged men and saw that they did not really want to do anything about it. I suggested what we should do was to get someone to take on this role and responsibility. They said there was no one interested so we should just forget about it. However, after a number of discussions, it was agreed we should hold a meeting at the Duke of Wellington pub on the following Sunday to decide what to do. Some union members were genuinely interested in keeping up the union, some were only interested in a good excuse for a drink on a Sunday.

The Sunday morning arrived and only 12 out of a possible 250 union members showed. When we discussed about how we could replace the rep who had gone AWOL no one wanted the job. In fact there was a suggestion that we should forget the whole situation. This didn't go down well with me and some others.

After about two hours it was quite clear that there were no candidates for the job. Further discussions resulted in the suggestion that I should take on the job, because I always had plenty to say when I was in the cafe in Birtley or the North Terrace pub at night. I reluctantly agreed to take on the job as a temporary arrangement until we held another meeting where we could appoint someone with a lot more experience than myself in the brewing industry. This was agreed.

On the bus journey home, I wondered just what I had let myself in for, with hardly any experience in the industry and even less on the subjects of unions, union relationships with management, working conditions and terms of employment. I had entered a new world that was virtually alien to me. I had a great deal to learn. I didn't sleep at all that night.

Later in the week, I went to the T&G's North East headquarters in Jesmond Road, Newcastle, an old-fashioned building which was in a rather run-down state. I met a man called Arthur Manners, the financial administrator, and I explained to him why I was there. I told him that Younger's Brewery union rep had left in a bit of a hurry and that I had been elected as the union rep and hadn't a clue as to what this entailed. He laughed out loud and said that's how everyone started.

He picked up a large ledger and told me that in the brewery

in Claremont Road there was only about 50 union members and many of those were in arrears with their weekly subscriptions. Between 250 and 300 people worked at the brewery.

Arthur Manners advised me to see Jack Dawson, the man responsible for transport in the brewery industry. I went upstairs, knocked on the door and met Jack Dawson for the first time. His was a poky office and there seemed to be books and documents all over the place. Jack was a very talkative man, about 6ft 2ins tall, and he told me about his position as trade group secretary and mentioned all the good things he had done for workers around the region and some of the good deals he had pulled off. I thought that was all well and good but I had never heard of anyone called Jack Dawson and I had certainly not heard of any deals done for brewery workers. He said he would offer me all the help and guidance that he could.

We walked downstairs to the main door and there stood a large bust. I asked Jack Dawson who it was.

"That's Ernie Bevin," said Jack. "The first general secretary of the T&GWU, which has a membership of 1.5million. He was the top man. A very powerful individual."

Ernie Bevin had been a drayman in his native Bristol and never was able to identify who his father was. He had gone through the branches and became general secretary of the union between 1922 and 1945. During the 1939-45 war Churchill had seconded him to the war cabinet to do a job involving industrial relations and to motivate the workforce to get behind the war effort. Ernie Bevin had also played a critical role in rebuilding the Labour Party after its collapse in 1931 when there was a split in the Party and Ramsay MacDonald led a Labour minority into a coalition with the Conservatives, a move Bevin bitterly opposed. In 1945, when Labour won the General Election, Ernie Bevin became Foreign Secretary in Clement Attlee's government

I didn't realise until then that someone from a trade union background could become such a prominent and influential figure nationally in British politics. For the first time I realised how strong the links were between trade unionism and the Labour movement

Jack Dawson went on to tell me about the current General Secretary of the T&G, Frank Cousins, who had been a wagon driver in Doncaster. He rose through the ranks, as Ernie Bevin had, to become the boss of the union in 1956.

Jack Dawson's brief history lecture on the T&G impressed upon me just how big and powerful the union was. Here I was, a branch representative of the union at Younger's Brewery, and I already felt like I belonged. I was looking forward to the challenge ahead. As I left the office in Jesmond Road, Jack gave me some rule books to swot up on, and a large number of application forms to try to boost recruitment.

The following day, when we had our regular after-work informal meeting in the North Terrace bar, everyone wanted to know what had happened at my meeting with the union officials. I indicated I wasn't going to tell everyone in the bar and we agreed to call another meeting in Newcastle the following Sunday in order for me to give them a full report and to draw up a list of complaints from the workers.

We met in the Duke of Wellington pub, the pub where my mother-in-law had put in a word for me with Younger's Brewery managers, and 30 people turned up. I had in front of me all the various rule books and we discussed how to move forward. We formed a union branch committee, agreed to hand out application forms to boost membership, and also agreed to draw up the list of complaints. The other new committee members said they would prefer that I carried out any negotiations with management.

During the next two weeks, people had heard of the list of complaints we were drawing up and many agreed to join the union. It was the first time any action had been contemplated to tackle the problems. When I received copies of the application forms, I took them straight along to the Jesmond Road office to make sure the union cards were given out the following day.

During my visits to the regional office I met Frank Burr, a mild-mannered man from Stockton who was the regional secretary of the T&G. He introduced himself to me and rather innocently I asked him about his job. I met Frank quite a few times over the next few weeks.

After about a month, virtually every worker at Younger's Brewery had joined the union. I didn't realise it at the time, but I was witnessing what was the start of mass unionisation within the brewing industry in the North East.

We had another meeting in the Duke of Wellington when more than 80 people attended and we spent the time drawing up the list of complaints, about 20 in all, covering terms and conditions of employment and safety and other important matters. I drafted up these complaints, took the list to Alan Davidson, who was then in charge of the transport and delivery side of the brewery and, eventually, my first formal meeting with management was arranged. I was aware that there was a lot at stake in this first meeting. The workers had high expectations and they were expecting me, their 25-year-old union representative, to deliver. I had to give it my best shot.

At the meeting, the brewery manager, George Robertson, Alan Davidson and two other company representatives sat around the table. I was accompanied by three colleagues, two from the transport division and one who worked inside the brewery

Mr Robertson opened up by saying he was disappointed that people had felt inclined to join the union as he saw himself as a sympathetic boss who tried to meet the employees' demands, even though they were sometimes over-demanding.

"I can appreciate what you are saying Mr Robertson," I said. "But people don't join trade unions because they want to, they do so for a reason, and there is a list of reasons here why people have decided to join."

I handed Mr Robertson the list of complaints and we began discussing each one at length. The meeting went on for more than three hours and the management decided they needed some time, at least seven days, to consider the issues.

At the end of the meeting, I thanked George Robertson for his time and shook his hand, and then made my way to the door. Mr Robertson called me back and told me he hoped that we could work together. He was doing all he could to enhance the brewery's reputation within the area, he said, and he hoped I would bear this in mind when I was representing the workers' views. What he didn't want in the brewery was any major conflict. When I left the office, one of my colleagues congratulated me on the way I had presented the case for the workers. "You should be on the stage," he said. I just smiled.

A week later, we met the management again to discuss the complaints list given to them and, much to my surprise, almost all of the complaints were going to be addressed. George Robertson then said if in future we had any complaints we should draw them to the management's attention as quickly as possible rather than wait so long and have such a long list. I suggested that a way to overcome this was for me to have a monthly meeting with management in order to resolve any problems that arise, and this was agreed.

George Robertson then asked me if there was anything else I wanted to raise with him.

"The general basic rate of pay needs looking at," I said, chancing my arm.

At our next union meeting at the Duke of Wellington

on the Sunday, I gave members a full report of the meeting with management and told them all their points were being dealt with. I also told them I had asked for a wage increase, which surprised everyone.

Two weeks later when we met the management again we were told that as a gesture or token of goodwill the company was increasing the basic rates of pay for the brewery and transport workers for the next 12 months.

Word soon spread around the brewery about the union's successful negotiations with the management, and everyone was delighted.

The success of the union at Younger's spread quite rapidly among a lot of the other breweries in the Newcastle and Durham area and many of the branches responded by trying to organise themselves into a more effective union force. Over the next few months we made some major inroads into the general terms and conditions of employment and the atmosphere within the company was quite positive.

In the brewery yard, in the offices and in the North Terrace bar, at the age of 25 and having worked at Bowburn Colliery only a few months earlier, my face was recognised by virtually everyone. My name, they said, was Joe Mills, the union man.

Chapter Thirteen

The merger of Younger's and McEwan's Breweries, which established Scottish Breweries Ltd., and the later merger between the Scottish brewer and Newcastle Breweries, which produced Scottish and Newcastle Breweries, meant the creation of the biggest branch of the Transport and General Workers' Union in the North of England, with a membership exceeding 1,600 people. Both mergers had been widely speculated on in the Press.

The T&G had also tried to organise a branch made up of all the drivers and other workers at Vaux Breweries in Sunderland, but the company responded by sacking all the workers who had joined the union and offered jobs to others in the town who would want to work for the company without the benefit of union membership. There was a pitiful sight in Sunderland when 400 workers were standing in queues waiting to apply for the jobs of those who had been sacked. I think Jack Dawson always had this in mind when he was asked to carry out recruitment at the various locations around the region.

After the merger of Younger's and McEwans, we suggested there should be parity of working conditions and pay for all the people now working for Scottish Breweries. This was resisted by the company's board of directors. We were told the terms of employment for McEwan's people were agreed by the Scottish brewers and Younger's was part of the Newcastle, Northumberland and Durham Brewers' Federation, which was effectively a cartel that set the terms and conditions of all the workers in the brewing industry.

I had numerous meetings with representatives of the previous McEwan's board and suggested to them that if they didn't agree parity, there would be serious problems. They seemed to dig in and wanted to continue to reject our claim.

In order to try to bring about a successful solution we held a very large meeting of union members from McEwan's and from Younger's workers in a large function room in a hotel ironcially owned by Newcastle Breweries, in the city's Haymarket. More than 500 people attended. After several delicate meetings with management afterwards, they agreed to our demands.

When the second merger happened, forming the company S&N Breweries Ltd, we entered yet another round of negotiations with brewery management who took the view that it would be about two years before the company settled down and they didn't not want any formal arrangements with the union. We rejected this argument and wanted to see the union grow into a large branch within the amalgamated company, which employed about 2,000 staff. The union developed and grew into a large branch in the amalgamated new company. We appreciated this was about 2,000 staff covered by the union.

The T&G began organising branch elections for the new company and decided the branch chairmanship and the position of branch secretary would have to be subject to an election.

I was in two minds about whether I should seek nomination as chairman of the merged branch as I realised it would be a stressful and pressurised job, which would put a great strain on my personal life.

I had enough on my plate as it was, with 600 members to look after. However, despite my reservations I was encouraged to put my hat into the ring for the branch chairmanship. Frank Burr, the regional secretary of the T&G, said I had the union's backing in the North East.

When the nomination list was circulated, I was surprised to find that two candidates had emerged from Newcastle Breweries. One was the current chairman of the branch and the other someone who worked internally. This had resulted in a split within the Newcastle Breweries vote. After the ballot closed and the votes counted, I was advised by the scrutineers that I had romped home. My votes were more than the two other candidates collectively. Here I was now, at the age of 26, with all the power and influence the position brought with it.

After the merger had taken place and the branch established, there was not a day passed when we were not meeting management in order to ensure parity of pay and conditions right across the company. A lot of the meetings were very acrimonious and tempers flared. The company did not want to concede. Frank Burr suggested I was being a bit too dogmatic in my attitude, a little too confrontational with the management, and that I should relax. I told him this was the only attitude they seemed to understand.

On one occasion it was suggested by the regional office of the T&G that the branch should be split into two. The reaction of the branch committee was that under no circumstances would we agree to the split.

During the intense negotiations, I was attending mass meetings almost every week, addressing hundreds of union members from the back of a wagon. Sometimes the workers were a little over ambitious in their demands. It meant more to tell the members the truth, even if it dented my popularity.

I had some major successes in the brewing industry in Newcastle and achieved some decent terms and conditions of employment for the T&G members. But there was always a tense situation around the brewery and anything could spark off some kind of dispute. We were becoming recognised in the region as a very militant union branch.

I discovered that certain conditions of employment applied to workers in Scotland but not in Newcastle. When I related this back to the members there was a demand for parity within the company. I was becoming a little tired with the members' constant demands but I met the company's representatives and put this argument to them. They rejected the claim out of hand.

After warning the company about how strong the members felt about the issue, and that industrial action could not be ruled out, the company was given five days to try and resolve the problem. It didn't and the whole brewery walked out in what was the biggest industrial dispute Tyneside had seen for many years.

I was forced to address a very large mass meeting of about 1,800 workers on Newcastle's Town Moor and the television cameras and reporters from newspapers and radio stations were there. I had to claim immediately that the union's claim for parity for pay and conditions was justified. The strike lasted for about four days and eventually the company finally conceded to our claim after a serious of acrimonious meetings with the board.

My job in S&N Breweries as chairman of the T&G branch continued to be very onerous and stressful. The problems that emerged had to be dealt with fairly quickly. The whole of the industrial relations scene at S&N was a hive of activity, with meetings here, there and everywhere.

There was also the reporting back to members, which meant travel to and from Scotland, and more meetings at nights, during the week and at weekends.

All this did have some impact on my domestic life because my two sons Adrian and Barry were now at school in Newcastle and their mother had to take full responsibility for them. Although I did try to share the responsibilities at weekends and go to Bowburn with my boys as often as I could to give their mother a break.

I was able to get one week away from S&N Breweries

for an intensive training course in Cirencester, organised by the T&G, for union activists from different parts of the country; dockers, Ford workers, transport company representatives, people who worked in engineering companies, and on motorway building and maintenance. The course was all about negotiating skills, how to obtain information from balance sheets and how to try to determine a company's progress. We were also taught debating skills and arguments that could be used with companies.

One thing I became more acutely aware of at Cirencester was how trade union representatives needed to be politically aware. We were taught all about the strong links between the unions and the Labour Party and the history and structure of the union. This in the main was all new to me.

I wasn't aware that the massive organisation I now worked for was controlled by lay people. The General Executive Council (GEC), a body of 35 people, was elected every two years and would meet to deal with the union business, its financial, political and industrial strategies, for one week every three months. The members of the GEC were elected from different parts of the country.

The T&G had its General Secretary, its Deputy General Secretary, a National Executive Officer and 12 national officials. Then there was the regional General Secretary and a Regional Secretary with 23 full-time officials, answerable to the regional committee made up of 30 lay people elected every two years from union branches.

The supreme policy making of the union was always set out at the biennial delegate conference, which was attended by about 1,000 delegates from regional branches and lasted for a week.

In the northern region there was five district union offices, with its head office in Newcastle.

At the Cirencester conference I was also taught about the union's political decisions by the executive and how it would try to try to influence the Labour Party.

I learned more about the Trades Union Congress (TUC), the structure of which both nationally and regionally mirrored to an extent the structure of the T&G, and about the importance of the union's block vote, the voting figure used at TUC and Labour Party conferences.

The T&G, the largest union in Britain, as you would expect, had a very large block vote which gave it a lot of clout both within the Labour Party and the TUC. I couldn't fully understand this system because it seemed totally undemocratic. How could they count the vote as one when there was so many different opinions within the organisations? I was told that was the way it had worked for many years. I couldn't help but feel that this would need to be changed sometime in the future if we were to be totally democratic.

At the biennial conference, I learned, the union's international, economic, political, financial and social policies were thrashed out. But if things changed within the weeks and months between the biennial conferences then the union's all powerful General Executive Council could step in, influenced, as ever, by the union boss, the General Secretary.

Over the years, the GEC of the T&G was left wing and the Labour Party was influenced by its policies, such as that on "banning the bomb", which General Secretary Frank Cousins took on as something of a personal crusade. The GEC had political views which were to the left and these were the types of policies pursued within the TUC and the Labour Party and the block vote used to great effect to get these policies accepted across the whole of the movement.

When I left Cirencester, I had a great deal to think about. I had never realised exactly what was going on in the name of the

T&G. The way I had been carrying out my job, it appeared, was very narrowly focused.

I met some very interesting union activists on the Cirencester course. Many of them had wild ideas about mass nationalisation, revolutions and following the Russian model of economics.

Early in 1963, the T&G advertised for a district secretary in the Carlisle office, which I applied for but was unsuccessful. The successful candidate was a full-time official from the Middlesbrough office who had a lot of experience and wanted to run his own show in Carlisle. When I left the interview, I made a mental note of the questions and wrote them down and decided to find out more about them.

A few months later another advert appeared for an organiser's job in Newcastle, involving recruiting new members and providing services to members at offices and factories across the region. During my interview, which lasted an hour, I suggested how we in the northern region could influence the Labour Party to try to bring much-needed improvements to the North East.

If we really had the power that we believed we had, as had been outlined to me on the course at Cirencester, then we should use this power politically to bring about changes in the North East's economic fortunes. I also said I thought the image of the T&G was very old fashioned, and we should try to recruit younger people into the union. This brought a smile to the interviewing panel and I wondered if I had overstepped the mark.

A week later, I received a letter from Frank Cousins telling me I had been successful in securing the job as union organiser for the T&G in Newcastle.

My days as the union branch chairman at Scottish and Newcastle Breweries, along with my employment at the company, were coming to an end, though I knew as T&G regional organiser

I would still be having dealings with the branch and the S&N management.

Frank Cousins had told me that the interviewing panel was particularly impressed by my youthful enthusiasm and exuberance, and that he hoped I would inject this into my job as regional organiser.

That I intended to do.

But when I walked into the T&G's head office in Jesmond Road, Newcastle, what I didn't realise was that I was starting out on a career in which I would witness 30 years of political intrigue, trade union power and influence.

And little did I realise that I would be rubbing shoulders with future Labour Party leaders, Royalty, international business figures and, in no small way, helping, with others, to put a little-known Labour Party member with high political aspirations on the road to Number 10 Downing Street.

Chapter Fourteen

The early 1960s saw the wind of change sweep across the country and nowhere, it seemed, were the changes more evident than in the North East, with local authorities, particularly Newcastle City Council, embarking upon major house clearance programmes, which saw the Victorian terraced slums replaced by gleaming, towering, high-rise council flats.

The era also witnessed the rapid growth in union membership and fierce competition between the big unions, conscious of the power of the block vote, to attract more new members, usually by fair means, but sometimes foul.

In my role as regional organiser for the T&G I was also becoming more actively involved within the Labour movement, trying to bring whatever influence I could to decisions that would impact not just on the lives of union members but on other, ordinary, working class North Easterners.

It was during this time that I met and worked alongside two powerful, charismatic and influential North East figures who rose to prominence in their respective fields through their own talents and leadership qualities, but who were also the architects of their own downfall. One was Mr Newcastle, T Dan Smith, and the other was Andrew Cunningham, the regional organiser of the T&G's biggest union rival in the North East, the General, Municipal and Boilermakers' union (the GMB).

Working in Newcastle for the Labour Party during the local council elections, I was in a committee room in Walker, with two or three other party workers, when T Dan Smith walked in. I was surprised to see how tall and immaculately dressed he was. He introduced himself to us and we had a brief discussion about what was happening in the local elections. T Dan was advised by a party organiser that people living in the high-rise flats in Walker were not turning out to vote. He suggested that he, along with two or three party activists, should visit the flats.

Parked in the street outside the committee room was Dan's car, carrying the personalised number plate Dan 1. We got in his car and travelled to the Walker flats. When we arrived at the flats, one of the organisers was asked to stay with the car, while Dan and I and two others went into the tower blocks to talk to the residents.

Residents who answered their doors recognised T Dan straight and one couple invited us in to tell us about the problems they had encountered in the flats, due to the city council. Dan was very eloquent and took a notepad from his pocket and said he would deal with the problems as soon as a he got back into the office the following day.

We knocked at another flat and the door was answered by a shabbily-dressed woman and her husband who had two equally shabbily-dressed children. As soon as they recognised T Dan Smith, we were invited in and the couple started talking about the problems in the flats, ranging from vandalism to repairs that needed doing.

When I looked around the room, I couldn't help but notice what a filthy place it was. I personally thought that it was the family's own neglect of the place that had caused the problems they were talking about. I noticed that in the middle of the dining room table there was a pile of dirty dishes littered with discarded food. The woman of the house asked if anyone wanted a cup of tea, and T Dan Smith said he would. "I always like a good cup of tea when I'm in Walker," he said.

The woman emptied the tea bags out of the pot, and, without cleaning it, put two more tea bags in, and topped the pot with hot water. She then emptied a dirty cup, didn't bother to wash it, and poured tea from the dirty pot into it, offering it to T Dan Smith.

He lifted the cup to his mouth and started drinking. "Hmm, that's the nicest cup of tea I've had in Walker for many years," he told the woman, whose face lit up with a smile.

When we left the flat and took the lift downstairs, I asked Dan why he had accepted the cup of tea.

"The tea was awful," he said. "But sometimes, as a politician, you have to do things that make people feel good, even if it is against your better nature."

Back at the committee rooms, we had tea from cups and saucers and I chatted to T Dan for a few minutes. He said that the unions and the Labour Party had a joint responsibility to help people like those we had met in the flats. He instilled in my mind quite clearly that it was a partnership between the trade unions and the Labour Party that could solve these problems.

I met Dan a number of times after this, but one of our meetings that sticks in my mind was when I was invited to attend a meeting of the transport sub-committee of Newcastle City Council to negotiate new terms and conditions for union members. I remember going into the room and there was a committee of about 15 people sitting. I presented my case to the 15 councillors and was then asked to leave the room during an adjournment. I was then invited back into the room for the decision. T Dan Smith had entered and was sitting at the end of the committee table.

The sub-committee chairman told me my case was worth supporting but it would have to go to the transport committee then the full council for approval.

T Dan Smith said: "Joe, tell your members when you

go back to work that they have secured their increase and it will be paid."

The sub-committee chairman turned to T Dan and said the application had to go before the transport committee, the establishment committee and then the full council.

Dan replied: "We're in charge of this council. I'm the leader and I'm telling Joe Mills he will get his increase with his members. We are not playing charades or trying to impress people with the committee structure. We're in charge and we will ensure they will get paid. It's justified and they will get it."

I left the room impressed by the straightforward approach of T Dan Smith and all of my members were delighted when they were told I had managed to secure them a pay rise through a strong personal recommendation from Mr Newcastle himself. I admired T Dan Smith and the way he operated. I was sad to see him jailed for corruption in later years for his involvement in the Poulson Affair.

Later, in 1968 when the T&G moved office from the old building in Jesmond Road to a refurbished building in Barrack Road, opposite St James's Park football ground, Frank Cousins performed the official opening. T Dan Smith was also in attendance as was the Lord Mayor of Newcastle, Roy Hadwin.

Another man jailed alongside T Dan Smith was my counterpart in the GMB, Andrew Cunningham, who was chairman of the North East Regional Labour Party, chairman of Durham County Council and was also on the National Executive of the Labour Party as national treasurer. He held a few other powerful and influential positions in the North East.

Andrew Cunningham was quite a character. I found him to be a very focused individual who knew exactly what he wanted from the union. The GMB was the largest union in the region and its officials understood that the more members you had in your union, the more members could affiliate with the ward branches of the Labour Party and the Constituency Labour Party.

The GMB could use its large block vote within the regional Labour Party, and that gave Andrew Cunningham a great deal of power. He wanted people who joined the GMB to become involved on the political scene, too.

His officials worked very much as a team and you always saw two or three of the officials operating together to recruit new members. It was known that Andrew Cunningham ruled the regional GMB like a rod of iron.

Of course, the T&G didn't have the same ethos as the GMB and lacked the political objectives when I first became an official. I aimed to change this over the years. I believed that the Andrew Cunningham style of leadership was the type that got things done and I secretly admired the way he operated.

At the time competition between the unions for new members was quite intense and we fought some fierce verbal battles at the factory gates, and elsewhere.

One battle for new members started when I received a phone call from an old school pal who was working at a factory in Annfield Plain. The GMB had been recruiting at the factory, where 200 people were employed, and had left application forms to collect two days later.

After hearing about this, I was at the factory gates within an hour and met my old school pal and asked him what had been happening. He told me two officials of the GMB had visited the factory and had spoken to the employer who had agreed the two officials could hand out application forms to the employees. One of the GMB organisers at the time was Jack Cunningham, the son of Andrew Cunningham, who later became a minister in the Government and Permanent Private Secretary to James Callaghan. I suggested to my friend that having the employer give the facilities to a union so easily and so quickly might not be in the workers' best interests.

I agreed to meet a lot of the workers that lunch time and put the same argument to them. Then I handed out T&G application forms and asked them to complete them there and then. I collected about 140 forms from the employees during the lunch period, went on to Newcastle and had the applications processed into union cards and took them back to the factory for 5pm, when the workers were finishing their shift. I handed the union cards out and welcomed them to the Transport and General Workers' Union.

The following day, I had to attend the regional Labour Party conference in Newcastle. Andrew Cunningham was chairing the meeting.

During the lunch break we got into conversation and he asked if I had had any success recently in attracting new recruits.

"Yes. I've just recruited 140 new members at a new factory in Annfield Plain," I said.

"You've got to be kidding," he said. "The GMB has just recruited those employees."

I suggested to him he might want to check his facts and, seeing how serious I was, he left the room with Jack Cunningham and another GMB organiser and returned ten minutes later.

When it dawned on him what had happened Andrew Cunningham was less than complimentary about my parenthood. The fact that someone had beaten his union to a membership coup, using similar tactics to those he had used in the past, was what concerned him.

I had started the job as the T&G's regional union organiser on June 17th 1963, which was my son's Adrian's birthday, and started working alongside Mike Chambers who introduced me to many employers and branch officials during my first few months in office.

I was also pleased after my first week in the union to be provided with a car to do my work across the region. This was quite a bonus attached to the job because I had never owned my own car. It would ease my problems travelling to Bowburn with the children, as well as organising people into the union and organising union branches across the North East.

When I got the car, I visited many industrial estates trying to recruit new members and I had some extremely odd experiences. I handed out 500 union application forms at a factory only to be handed them all back by the boss the next day, wrapped in elastic bands. None of them had been completed. Undeterred, I went back to the factory and handed out leaflets about a meeting I had arranged the following Friday at a local pub. I sat in the pub expecting masses of people to arrive but at 6.30pm I was still waiting. By 7pm still no one had turned up so I decided to go down to the factory to see what was going on. Unusually, all the workers had been told they needed to work compulsory overtime!

Eventually, I got most of the workers signed up, but the company refused to recognise the union and it resulted in a seven-day strike. The company went out of business seven months later, not because of union activity but simply because of bad management.

By contrast, at Welch's Sweet Factory in North Shields (owned by the family of Coronation Street actress Denise Welch) I was standing outside trying to recruit the workers when the chairman and managing director of the firm helped me to carry out my job, by arranging a mass meeting which I addressed, encouraging his staff to collect the completed application forms, and then, when I told him about the need to collect union dues, he advised they could be deducted at source. I later learned that Mr Welch, a very shrewd businessman, had heard of a situation in the Midlands where five separate unions were recruiting at the same factory, causing a bit of a mess, so he preferred dealing with only one – and in this case it was the T&G.

The relationship we had with Welch's sweet factory over the years was probably one of the best between any union and employer in the country. When the union or the Labour Party ran charitable events, Welch's factory even provided us with lollipops and other sweets for the children.

That single-union agreement was a coup for the T&G, but another, agreed between the T&G and an American company, Patchogue-Plymouth Ltd, who set up a man-made fibre plant in Consett, County Durham, became the first "pace-setter" agreement in the North East, according to the local press.

When the company was looking to establish in Consett, officials met a man called John Sudder, then the chairman of Consett Urban District Council and a fitter at the local colliery. The company representatives from Indiana thought that as chairman of the council. John Sudder had executive authority and they were impressed by the way he treated them and how he addressed some of their problems.

He was asked to visit America to have a look at the company's major plant and while he was there he attended the local baptist's church on the Sunday. John, who was a lay preacher, was asked to give a sermon and he did so and impressed everyone. He became the industrial relations director of the new company in Consett. He accepted the position but had no experience at all of industrial relations at that level. He recruited about 200 people to the company, many from the colliery where he had worked. However, when all the workers were taken on, there was still no union to represent them.

I got a phone call from John Sudder who said he had seen me in the paper and on television, that he would like me to go and see him, and that he wanted to recognise one union because he had recognised only one union – the NUM – when he worked in the colliery.

When I met him, he gave me a single piece of white paper and asked me to draft the terms and conditions for the employees, the procedure agreements and also the various recognition clauses which recognised the union and suggested within the agreement that everyone should be members of the T&G. We virtually had the single union agreement, the first single union agreement in the North East.

Our union had quite a good blitz on the people who worked at supervisory level within the bus industry. Bus drivers, in the main, were all members of the T&G, both in the private sector and the public sector, but the inspectors who worked on the buses owned and run by Newcastle City Council were not fully organised by any means. I decided to try to use the bus branches to encourage the inspectors to become members, and we were successful in this campaign because we pointed out that many of the bus drivers were getting more money than the inspectors, what with overtime and perks. I put in an application to Newcastle City Council for all the inspectors in Newcastle who worked for the municipal bus industry to have a pay increase.

But, unlike industry, where you would negotiate with the local managing director, I had to go in front of a full council transport committee. At the time, the committee chairman was Neville Trotter, now Sir Neville Trotter.

I wasn't too sure what to expect but I had a tip-off from one of the Labour councillors on the costs to the authority of any pay rise. He gave me the specific figures that the council had drawn up.

When I went into the committee to present the case, I was accompanied by three or four inspectors who were new to the trade union game and who wanted to see how I performed. There was about 24 councillors sitting there and various officers and I was invited by Neville Trotter to present the case. At the end of my presentation, I was asked by Neville Trotter if I had any idea what this would cost the local authority if they re-graded the inspectors from grade two to grade three. I asked him how many inspectors they had on the books. He said a certain figure and I pretended to do a quick calculation and came out with the exact cost to the council. I could see the look of surprise on Neville Trotter's face. What about grade three to grade four? He asked. Again, I gave the impression I was doing a quick calculation and came up with the exact figure. Neville Trotter, who was a chartered accountant, said he had never seen anyone calculate figures so quickly.

My activities in the union made the headlines in the local press many times and, as a result of the publicity, I was contacted by many people wanting to join the union. One call came from a group of air stewardesses at BKS Airways, the private operator from Newcastle Airport, which is now part of British Airways. We had a meeting at my office in Newcastle and, to put some pressure on the company, a local newspaper reporter and photographer were invited along. The photo taken of me sitting at the conference table surrounded by these very glamourous stewardesses appeared in the newspapers the following day.

I got a call from the personnel director of the company in London, asking me for an immediate meeting in order to resolve the problems. Clearly he was unhappy with the story but also the press picture. I suggested I could meet him at some place outside of Newcastle or in London but stressed I did not want any pressure brought on to the stewardesses because of their approach to me as a union official. He said the company reserved the right to do what they wanted with their employees. I told him I reserved the right to speak to my members who were fuel delivery drivers who would be sympathetic with the claim from the stewardesses. An agreement was reached and the air stewardesses won their claim for union recognition.

I was learning that there was always more than one way to skin a cat, and the local press was often a powerful medium to get the right message across.

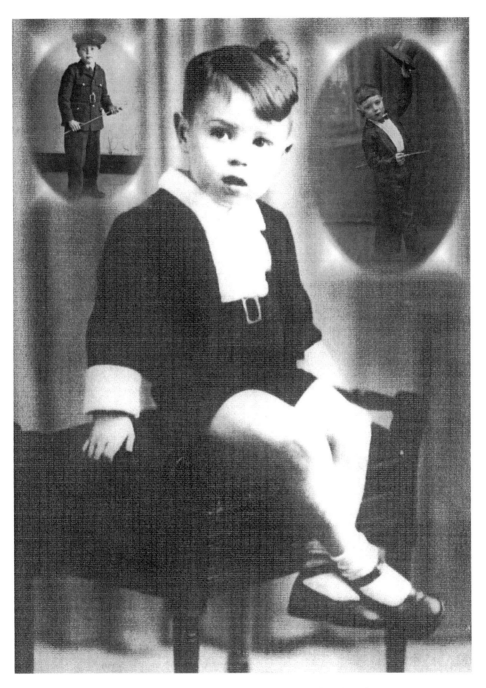

A two year old Joe, centre, and early days in the show group

Performing at the Windsor Tattoo, above. In the Army, R.E.M.E., below.

Joe launching the 'Back to Jarrow March' and, inset, Regional Secretary

Meeting the Leaders of the Labour Party

Left: Prime Minister, James Callaghan, Joe, Joanne & Lirena, Cardiff 1977.

Right: Jack Jones, Frank Cousins & Moss Evans.

Left: Roy Hattersley, Deputy Leader, Labour Party.

Below:
Dennis Healy

Above: John Prescott, Deputy Prime Minister

Joe, the Union Leaders & the Politicians

Left: Greeting H.M. the Queen at the opening of the International Centre for Life, Newcastle.

Right: With the Princess Royal, Garden Festival, Gateshead.

Lirena and I talking with Princess Diana at the opening of an older persons home in Walker, Newcastle.

Joe & the Royal Family

With my Honourary Doctorate from Sunderland University, and
with Lord Glenamara, Vice Chancellor, University of Northumbria.

Receiving my O.B.E. from H.R.H. Prince Charles
and outside the Palace with my family.

Lucy-Ann, left, and Joanne, below,
after receiving their degrees.

Left:
Son Barry and
grandson Scott

Above: Son Adrian

Above: Visiting family in Perth.
Adrian, Jaqui, Joanne, Lirena, Lucy-Ann & me.

My family

Left: Nephew Michael Clark

Father Larry

Mother Mary

Grandmother, Annie Bell.

Lirena's mother Amy.

With Lirena

Our wedding day with
Giles and Lizanne Radice

With mother, me & aunt Meggie

Chapter Fifteen

The power of the individual trade unions was always a matter of concern within the North East. Within the region there was a TUC trade union advisory committee, established so that full-time officials could meet to discuss matters of general interest. What they also did was to elect an executive committee who nominated people for membership of various statutory bodies. It was very much a committee with a power to put people on to various boards. Not many people attended these advisory committee meetings and a cabal started to rule the roost.

One day, all the officials of the T&G were told we were to have a joint meeting with the GMB officials at their office in Thorn House on the West Road in Newcastle. We didn't know why this meeting had been called but it soon became apparent when we arrived. We were told the executive committee of the trade union advisory committee was very much biased towards certain unions. The GMB and the T&G, the two largest unions in the region, were not being given a fair crack of the whip.

It was the general view of Andrew Cunningham, of the GMB, and Frank Burr, our regional secretary at the time, that something should be done to sort the matter out.

It was agreed that we would go en masse to the next advisory committee meeting, which happened to be its Annual General Meeting, and we would nominate either a GMB or a T&G member for every seat that was available. The meeting was held in the

Co-op Hall in Newgate Street, Newcastle, and the chairman of the meeting was Danny McGarvey, the boilermakers' leader, and next to him was Jim Harper, the UCAT regional secretary and honorary secretary of the committee. When they saw the GMB and T&G officials entering the meeting en masse, alarm bells started to ring.

After about five minutes of reading minutes the meeting was opened and nominations were called for the 12 positions on the executive. As agreed at the meeting between the GMB and T&G officials, all of the positions that were identified were nominated for by both of our organisations. We succeeded in getting our members on to all 12 positions on the executive.

The final questions were on the position of the chairman and the honorary secretary. Andrew Cunningham recommended that the chairman of the committee, Danny McGarvey, should continue. Frank Burr recommended that the secretary, Jim Harper, should stay in the post. This was seen as very much a gesture of goodwill. It was pointed out to them both that if in the future the GMB and the T&G were not treated fairly then there would be an en masse delegation to the next Annual General Meeting and a mass clear out. It was a fairly acrimonious meeting and after it closed, the arguments continued for the next hour or so.

When I left the meeting, I knew that I had witnessed the raw power of the region's two largest unions at work. I could see why it had been done, but I thought there were other ways it could have been handled.

After the meeting when we went into a local pub for a drink there was a mood of triumphalism. Personally, I felt uncomfortable, thinking a more conciliatory and positive attitude should have been adopted between unions if we were to establish a good strong trade union movement in the North to improve the terms and conditions of members and employees.

We had to try to enhance the North East as a region and

needed to find ways for the unions to work together rather than giving each other a bloody nose.

The National Union of Public Employees (Nupe), now called Unison, mainly tried to attract members from the public sector, but so did the GMB, and the two unions were in constant conflict. Nupe's style and authority changed when Rodney Bickertstaffe became the Regional Secretary some years later. He was assisted by Tom Sawyer, now Lord Sawyer, who became the Deputy Regional Secretary. Both Rodney Bickerstaffe and Tom Sawyer served on the northern regional executive of the Labour Party.

In 1963, after I was appointed a full-time official for the T&G, I was able to attend the Labour Party Conference in the autumn. The Newcastle office was able to send two delegates, so I went along with Mick Chambers. When we arrived at the conference hall, I sat directly behind Frank Cousins, the T&G's General Secretary. I have to admit I was very much in awe of the man. As the leader of Britain's biggest union, he had a lot of power.

Some weeks later, Frank Cousins visited the Carlisle district of our union and I was invited over there to be part of the official visiting party. Frank visited a number of factories, talking to the employees and the management and I saw first hand how he operated. He was very similar in style and knowledge to T Dan Smith. I thought he and T Dan Smith had much in common. After the visits, we adjourned to out hotel and about eight of us had dinner. We were talking about the North East and some of our traditions and I mentioned leek growing, knowing for a fact Frank Cousins was a keen gardener.

I mentioned the huge leeks that were grown in the North East and the big prizes that could be won in competitions. I could see Frank Cousins looking at me in some disbelief. I tried to encourage some of the guests around the table to confirm what I was saying but in a mischievous way they said I must be exaggerating about the size of the leeks. It was all good banter. Frank said he wouldn't mind a seeing a couple of these enormous leeks and, before he left for London, asked if I could send a couple to him on the train.

Fortunately, the leek shows were being held in the next few weeks and I used my influence with a couple of friends in the North East clubs to obtain two very large prize-winning leeks. Two days later, one of my colleagues was going to London on business and I asked him to take the leeks to Frank Cousins' office.

Three days later, I got a letter from Frank Cousins, on his personal paper, thanking me for sending him two of the biggest spanking specimens of leek he had ever seen in his life.

Two or three weeks later, one of the members of the General Executive Council was telling me that during the adjournment of the meeting Frank Cousins had mentioned that he had started to grow leeks and gave some of them to his gardening friends in the southern counties.

I thoroughly enjoyed the Labour Party conference in 1963 and was impressed by the speakers from the unions. Frank Cousins was a shining example. Some of the issues the delegates hotly debated, such as high unemployment, social deprivation, poverty and social exclusion were very prevalent in the North East. I again thought about what T Dan Smith had told me in Walker; that the unions could not tackle these issues on their own, but combined with the Labour Party they could become a power for good.

After the conference, I found myself becoming more drawn in to Labour Party activities as well as my trade union work, which again placed tremendous pressure on my family and social life.

During my early involvement in the Labour Party in the North East, I concluded that every local ward of the Labour Party and every local council believed the world began and ended in their own backyards. Labour councillors were making efforts and strides to improve the lot of the people they represented, but there appeared to be no liaison or co-operation between the local authorities to act in a stronger, co-ordinated and unified way. Many of the problems in the North East, it seemed to me, resulted from the local authorities not working together.

This continued for several years. We had some very strong and powerful Labour leaders in the local councils but their authority was very much within the geographical area they served. Many of the council leaders socialised together but there was never any real attempt in those early days for them to work together on behalf of the whole northern region. There were barriers between the local councils and it took a long while to bring those barriers down. Visionaries like T Dan Smith tried to break the mode, but met with difficulties.

My view at the time, and a view I still hold strongly, is that the pain and suffering of individuals who have no jobs or suffer from other types of deprivation in New Kyo is no different to the situation thousands of other people found themselves in; in Walker, Birtley, Sunderland, Darlington or Middlesbrough. I felt that if we all worked together collectively, rather than restricting our vision to improving our own territory, the whole of the North East could benefit in some way. The unions, and the Labour Party, had a major part to play in this renaissance.

In 1967, Frank Burr, the regional secretary of the T&G, collapsed and died in Newcastle Central Station. He lived in Stockton and often took the train to and from work.

The General Executive Council went through the whole process of selecting Frank Burr's replacement and several hats were thrown into the ring; one in particular I disapproved of, because I thought the candidate would cause untold damage to the relationships between the unions in the region. The job went to Mick Chambers, which delighted me, and I succeeded Mick as Trade Group Secretary, which gave me more clout within the organisation and freed my hands to become more involved in thrashing out new agreements for members and to become more active in Labour Party affairs.

I had my own personal vision for the North and believed the Labour Party and the unions could bring about change for the better. It was a question now of persuading others to jump on board.

Chapter Sixteen

I pulled myself back into the affairs of the brewing industry in a very big way and was met head on with one of my biggest challenges as a union official to date. It involved a very militant branch of the union, a £1million pay-out, three Newcastle pubs, and a racehorse called Brigadier Gerard.

The brewery was growing in many areas and was fast becoming one of the biggest brewers in Great Britain. It did many deals with suppliers in other parts of the country in order to ensure that its products were spread as far and wide as possible with reciprocal arrangements with other brewers and companies.

The brewery decided that because of the volume of traffic, in other words the number of beer wagons, going to London, it would transfer all of its bulk beer on to freight liners, transporting it to London and other areas from the rail freight depot at Follingsby. This meant that all of the work previously done by the long-distance drivers would stop and the drivers would be offered jobs within the brewery.

The shop stewards and members of the very militant branch of the transport section at S&N Breweries, the 8-223 branch, resisted the move. They were well-paid long-distance lorry drivers and wanted to remain such.

After many meetings, a proposal was put forward that any savings the company made by switching long-distance deliveries to rail rather than road should be shared with the transport workers. The company resisted the proposal. Neither side would budge, so the matter was taken to arbitration.

At the arbitration panel, I argued the case for the branch members saying if the company was to use freight at Follingsby for the beer deliveries then this was a productivity factor that needed to be identified as benefit received by everyone. At the time the Government was trying to promote productivity deals around the country so that there would be better use of machinery, manpower and working hours. This deal, I suggested, fell within the Government's thinking on the issue.

About two weeks later, a letter was received by the brewery and the union to say that the arbitrator had found in favour of the union. This was a bitter blow for the company but was met with jubilation by the members of the transport branch. We met the company the next day and it agreed the no-limit agreement should be put in operation.

Some drivers were given alternative employment, so they really didn't lose anything other than the additional payments for them driving to London and back.

The transport branch was constantly on the look out for ways of enhancing members' earnings, even if it meant breaking rules to do so. S&N Brewery did a deal with Schweppes and the deal was that Schweppes would distribute S&N products within its outlets in London and S&N would deliver Schweppes products within Tyneside and other areas of the North East.

When this deal was made known to the draymen of the 8-233 branch, they argued that it fell within the productivity deal already agreed by the arbitrator. I explained to the transport drivers that this was really taking things a bit too far, even though I understood their argument. I put the case back to the company that this deal should now be incorporated into the deal when it was agreed to use the rail freight depot at Follingsby. The company refused to concede and the matter was taken back to arbitration for clarification. The brewery argued that the Schweppes deal was separate. The tribunal chairman, after listening carefully to all the arguments, concluded that the deal agreed by the earlier chairman of the arbitration panel was not just a one-off deal for one year but a continuing deal.

The brewery management was shell-shocked. The company had to take the tribunal decision on board. The members of the transport branch of the union were, naturally, elated that they had again won the day.

Every year, the draymens' committee received a cheque from the company and the shop stewards would divvy out the cash to the draymen and drivers based on their time in the job. Everyone in the branch got a substantial amount. It was also agreed that they would create a branch fund and some of the annual windfall from the company went into this fund. The branch became very wealthy.

After three or four years of the productivity agreement being in operation, the chairman of S&N Breweries, Peter Balfour, asked for a meeting to talk about the ongoing situation. He presented me with figures and said the brewery was considering opening a brewery in Washington, Tyne and Wear, which would cost £40million but because of the militant attitude of the transport branch in Newcastle it was not prepared to make this investment. The company felt the branch was totally out of control and that neither the union nor the union's executive were able to do anything about it.

I explained to the chairman in great detail that the decisions of the arbitration board were not mine and that the brewery had agreed to adhere to the decisions. During the conversation, I was asked by the chairman what it would cost to buy this deal out. I said I would put this to the branch at its next meeting.

About two weeks later there was a special meeting called in Newcastle and almost every member of the branch attended. I explained the situation to the members and the company's concern about the militant attitude of the branch and went on to suggest that the company was about to invest £40million in a brewery in Washington but had decided against it because of the militancy of the branch.

This went down with hoots of laughter; the branch members knew they had the upper hand. I then asked them what they would accept from the company who wanted to buy out the deal. After a lengthy discussion, three propositions were put forward. One was that the brewery pay the draymen £1million to share out among the workers. Alternatively, they would accept three pubs in Newcastle which they would identify and run on a co-operative basis, and, thirdly, the brewery could buy them a racehorse, called Brigadier Gerard. I couldn't believe what I was hearing, but the members stood firm and said that was the deal.

I related this back to the board of S&N Breweries and the directors threw up their hands in disbelief. There was a meeting in Edinburgh with the full board and I was rather amused when one of the Scottish landed gentry directors asked in a very vague way whether or not Brigadier Gerard was for sale. He was given a rather wry look by the chairman for such a naive question.

The General Secretary of the T&G, Jack Jones, who had taken over from Frank Cousins, rang me and asked what the hell was going on. He was being asked how the branch had managed to get itself into such a strong negotiating position; asking for a £1million payout, a racehorse or three pubs to be shared among approximately 250 drivers.

During this tense and very difficult period, I was invited to lunch by one of the directors of S&N Breweries, who I knew was acting very much on his own. He said to me the company was concerned about this impasse. The company had decided against the £40million brewery investment in Washington because of the draymens' and drivers' attitude. The suggestion of £1million was outrageous, he said, and three pubs were out of the question. During our conversation he made it plain that he would make it worth my while if I could get the branch members to change their minds.

When he said that, I put my knife and fork on the table, stood up and walked over to another table where a senior manager from another company was sitting.

"I want you to remember this date," I told him. " I have just had an improper proposition put to me by that gentleman over there and I am now going to leave the premises."

I left the restaurant, went back to the office, and spoke to Mick Chambers about what had happened. He was as horrified as I was and we immediately rang Jack Jones and related the conversation to him. He was furious.

There were phone calls to members of the S&N board from Jack Jones and, ultimately, we suspended negotiations with S&N Breweries across the whole country until the matter could be resolved.

After many discussions, the director concerned acknowledged he had done what I had suggested and apologised in writing to everyone concerned.

The transport branch was fully aware of what was going on and when I related the result of what had happened to them at a meeting, I was given a round of applause.

After more and more meetings, the company offered a very substantial amount of money which the draymen accepted, but once again the cash was top sliced to put into the branch. We as a union were very concerned about the size of the branch fund, but there was little we could do about it.

Not long after the branch's success, I was invited by members to a meeting in a Newcastle pub with 12 shop stewards. I didn't know what they were after but decided that I was growing increasingly impatient with their selfish attitude and militancy and the best form of defence would be attack. Before they had the opportunity to tell me what they wanted, I launched a tirade of criticism against every one of them, telling them I was sick and tired of the way the branch was operating, that the shop stewards were causing problems and they were not trade unionists at all, they were just out to feather their own nests.

"Now," I concluded. "What the hell do you want!"

After my tirade there was a deafening silence. Then all the shop stewards started grinning. One of the shop stewards, John Shaw, stood up, walked towards me and opened a box.

"On behalf of the branch I would like to present you with this watch for all the good work you have done for us and the leadership you have given us," he said.

I just stood there, open-mouthed. For the first time in my union work I was literally lost for words.

One of the effects of all the trouble between the branch and the S&N brewery resulted in me coming up against a lot of resistance from employers in my efforts to secure negotiating rights. We tried to secure an agreement with Nimmos Breweries, which became Whitbread, and Camerons Brewery in Hartlepool, but had to strike to gain union recognition.

An article in the trade paper, the Morning Advertiser, written by Ted Elkins, didn't help the case. His article, which ran across a full page, said: "Look Out the Fastest Gun Alive is in town and he is on the prowl." The article continued: " The man's name is Joe Mills. Say his name among any brewery managers in the North East of England and their reactions will be surprising. It's like telling an Indian village a man-eating tiger is on the prowl or telling a western cowboy town the fastest gun is calling."

Ted Elkins said this was the reaction from brewery managers he had found at the mention of my name. In his article, he added: "They say he just insults brewers to get their backs up, the bigger the brewer the bigger the insult. If he can upset them, he can defeat them."

All this did not help my bid to secure union recognition in other brewing companies. Organisational and negotiation rights were only secured with Nimmos after a strike. Eventually, after some time, we secured union rights with almost all the breweries in the North East. The only one brewery where that didn't happen was Vaux Breweries in Sunderland, but an agreement was reached with the T&G at a later stage.

The shop stewards of the S&N 8-233 branch were still causing problems for the union and something needed to be done. An opportunity arose when they arranged a meeting to pass a vote of no confidence in one of the branch officials.

At the special meeting, all the members wanted to do was hurl abuse at anyone who took to the platform. After about an hour, after I had read them the riot act, I told them that was it, I was closing the branch down, even though I did not have the authority to do so. The branch members didn't realise I didn't have this authority. I left the meeting with verbal abuse ringing in my ears.

As expected, the branch pursued me for many months, culminating in a case at Leeds Crown Court. The judge decided in my favour and also decided I could seek costs from the shop stewards' committee. I decided not to pursue costs as this would have caused personal hardship to some of the members. Afterwards, the branch was not reformed and its members dispersed to different locations around the North East.

I became chairman of Scottish and Newcastle Breweries negotiating committee with the task of negotiating to keep or improve the terms and conditions of S&N employees throughout the country. Wherever there was an issue to be dealt with, either myself or David Cairns, from the Scottish office, had to become fairly well-involved.

On one occasion, we were told that one of the shop stewards employed by S&N in Belfast had been sacked for throwing bottles from the back of his wagon. He had obviously been under the influence of alcohol. The shop steward was actively involved with the Provos and the officer concerned with the depot at the time, Eddie Carling, was having great difficulty in getting the man reinstated.

Not many people realised that within Belfast, and within the brewing industry particularly, we had to ensure that 50 per cent of employees were Catholics and 50 per cent Protestant. It was a policy that had to be strictly adhered to. David Cairns and I were told to go to Belfast to try to sort the problem out.

David was a Glasgow catholic and what with me being a protestant, with a slight association with the Salvation Army, we stood on opposite sides, as far as Belfast was concerned, of the sectarian divide.

We arrived in Belfast late evening and were taken to the Stormont Hotel, where we had a quick sandwich and a beer before retiring to bed. When I got into my room, I noticed at the side of the bed there was a brown paper parcel. This aroused my suspicions and I alerted the receptionist who came up and opened the bag. It contained six small cans of lager with a compliment slip, left by the brewery.

The following day, we had talks with Eddie Carling and an interview with the shop steward at the centre of the problem and it was clear he was not prepared to do any deals with us. Our difficulty was that if we pressed it only half the workforce would have gone on strike and the other half would have stayed at work. It was a delicate issue that took a great deal of time to resolve.

That night, Eddie Carling came and had a beer with us and suggested that we might want to visit a Belfast pub which was frequented by a local MP. We agreed but discussions went on until late in the evening and we didn't make it to the pub.

The next morning while we were sitting in the hotel having

breakfast Eddie Carling came in and appeared to be a little flustered. He asked if we had seen the local papers that morning. We said no. It became clear that between 8.30pm and 9pm the night before – the time we were due to meet Eddie in the Belfast pub – a number of people had entered the bar hoping the MP would be there and raked the place with a Sten gun, causing a great deal of damage.

After breakfast, David Cairns got a phone call and told us he would see Eddie and I at the brewery later in the day. When we got to the brewery depot at about 10am, David Cairns had yet to arrive. He turned up at midday and said the matter with the sacked shop steward had been resolved.

I flew back to England on a different aircraft to that of David Cairns but the next day I rang him and asked how the hell he had persuaded the shop steward to resign. Without going in to too much detail he explained that money had changed hands. He explained that the community was looking for some form of payment if the shop steward left the company and David had negotiated the amount. I didn't ask too many questions, but it appeared this was not an unknown practise in Belfast.

Another thing I was told while in Belfast was about a brewery wagon being hi-jacked about once a month with all the beer crates and barrels on board stolen. The police and the Army were made aware of this, but, I was told, the monthly hi-jackings continued. I got the impression this was some form of protectionism for community activists, a monthly event the company was prepared to accept, but when I spoke to S&N management they would not confirm this.

About a week after my visit to Belfast, I was sent a brown envelope in the post which arrived at my office in Newcastle. It turned out to be a letter from one of the shop stewards, who represented the other side of the community, with a flag of the UDA thanking me very much in my efforts to get rid of

137

the shop steward. The writer assumed, wrongly, that I was on their side.

Chapter Seventeen

The power in the hands of a few leading lights within the trade union movement and within the Labour Party would always bring with it allegations of favouritism, nepotism, impropriety and even corruption.

I was pleased that in my position I may have heard wild rumours and spurious allegations but there was never any evidence to back up the claims. Power brings with it influence and responsibility, but it also produces envy in political rivals.

All that changed, however, when I moved with my family to Vigo in Birtley, on the border of Gateshead and Washington, and joined the Birtley ward Labour Party. Local councillors knew a top union official had moved on to their patch, and they wanted me to play a full and active part in the Labour Party's ward activities.

I didn't want to become too involved because of the pressure of work and needing to spend time with my family, but it was always difficult to turn down invitations to speak at various functions.

My involvement within the Birtley Labour Party and later Chester-le-Street Constituency Labour Party led me into getting into things I never thought I would be involved in at the time.

There was constant rumours around the area about corruption. Backhanders being accepted by some local councillors in return for dispensing favours to local builders. Rumours were rife, but evidence was hard to come by.

One of my first jobs at the Birtley Labour Party was to act as the agent on behalf of the district and parish council elections. The Lib Dems had been making some inroads into Birtley and one of the leading Lib Dems in the area was Kathy King, who was a very go-ahead and very energetic councillor.

When I was asked to be the local agent, I asked for total authority within the job to deal with publicity and policy statements that would be issued.

I had a broadsheet newspaper printed in Birtley outlining the biographical details of the six candidates for the local district and parish councils and headlined the paper "Six of the Best". It was a high profile campaign and our six candidates were duly elected.

I was enjoying my involvement with the local Labour Party but the nagging rumours of corruption would not go away. One of the rumours was that some councillors on Chester-le-Street Rural District Council were somehow involved.

One of the specific allegations was that a builder had bought 13 houses from the National Coal Board, near Craghead, which were in a dilapidated condition and in danger of falling down. The builder bought each house for £50 on the proviso that they would be demolished and the rubble used for hardcore in his other building work.

However, once the deal had been done the builder sought planning permission from the council to refurbish the properties, which went totally against the principle of the sale by the NCB. Permission was granted and the local builder renovated the properties, selling each for more than £13,000, which gave him a handsome profit.

Another rumour began circulating about alleged dodgy dealings over a development in Birtley behind one of the big petrol filling stations. There was a large area of land which a company tried to acquire to build a very large supermarket. The local traders lobbied against the plan and it was kicked out by the council. The land then stood empty for about six months.

A number of people within the local Labour Party were so concerned about the rumours of corruption, we formed ourselves into a small, secret, committee, intending to clean up the party's image locally. I was able to use my union's research team to look at company accounts, discover who sat on various boards and see what interests councillors might have in the company concerned or associated organisations. We acquired some interesting information.

The big problem was how to confront the councillors concerned and ask them the direct questions, without opening ourselves up to a libel or slander writ. The idea was we should try to raise the whole issue in the Labour Party locally to have an open and frank discussion, within the ward and the constituency.

The committee we started was called CAPP (Campaign Against Political Pollution) . No one knew who was on the committee. There was about six of us and we used to meet up in secret and draw up all sorts of newsletters, not naming anyone, but referring to corruption in the broadest sense stressing the need for the issues to be raised properly, in the proper forum. This rattled a few councillors and others.

The BBC's Newsnight team had dug around and discovered a little more about the problems at Craghead and the builder who bought the properties for demolition. They were also aware of the builder's links with the chairmen's committee in Chester-le-Street and one night they dedicated a full programme to the subject, alleging possible corruption in the town. I was interviewed by the Newsnight team and asked if I had any evidence at all to give to the BBC. I said I was as surprised as anyone else about the rumours circulating in the area. My interview went out across the national network and I was portrayed as a kind of knight in shining armour, trying to clean up the local party. For the next few weeks, I received many abusive telephone calls and threatening letters and suggested I should clamp up rather than create problems.

Some months later at the Chester-le-Street Constituency Labour Party meeting, I heard there was to be a recommendation that the land behind the petrol filling station in Birtley was to be given to a new developer. The proposal had gone through one of Durham County Council's planning committees. I couldn't understand why, after such a short space of time since the supermarket development was thrown out, a new development had been granted planning permission with what appeared to be little debate and no consultation.

I knew the name of the development company and used my union's research department in London again to find out what it could. The new company was run by none other than the local builder behind the controversy at Craghead and two local councillors, who had failed to declare an interest when the plan went before the Durham County Council planning committee, were on the company's board of directors.

When the subject was raised at the CLP meeting I asked who the development company was, having armed myself with 200 copies of the report on the company I had received from the research department. A councillor responded by saying he didn't know who the developer was and had not even asked during the planning committee meeting.

I produced the reports naming the developer, the local builder who was running the company, and the names of the two councillors sitting on its board. The revelations went down like a bomb at the meeting and some of those involved threatened to sue me. I gave them seven days to prove that the information was wrong, but nothing was forthcoming.

The information was picked up by the Newsnight team and the local police, who launched an investigation. One of the councillors involved with the development company was jailed. Another councillor was jailed but on appeal had his conviction quashed.

One of the ironies of the case was that during the trial one of the builders had been accused of sending hampers of groceries and other goodies to the home of one of the councillors, but right through the trial the councillor denied it.

Some years later, when the whole thing died down, I was contacted by someone who lived in the same street as the councillor, who told me he had received many hampers over many months, had an idea what was going on, but kept his head down and said nothing. He certainly enjoyed the good life for a period – the hampers had been sent to the wrong address! I remember seeing this man, who I agreed I would not name, at a local pub when the case first emerged, smoking the finest cigars while enjoying a drink with friends.

Through my involvement with the Campaign Against Political Pollution, and other matters locally, I was beginning to make a name and reputation for myself within the Labour Party in Chester-le-Street

When Norman Pentland, the MP for Chester-le-Street, died, a sponsored member of the NUM, a list was drawn up of the potential candidates who might replace him as the Honourable Member for Chester-le-Street. It was rumoured that Andrew Cunningham wanted the seat for a GMB member.

Mick Chambers, the regional secretary of the T&G, told me that Jack Jones, the General Secretary, wanted me to put my nomination in for the Chester-le-Street seat. I told Mick I had no wish to become an MP and that I enjoyed the job that I was doing. He suggested I should speak to Jack Jones on the phone. I did so from his office, and I said to Jack the same I had said to Mick. I did not want to be an MP. Jack told me I wouldn't become an MP. He said he had heard Andrew Cunningham was aiming to take the seat from the NUM for the GMB, but if I put my name forward we could have some tactical voting amongst the unions to try to return the seat to an NUM delegate.

I allowed my name to go forward. It was among 11 nominations.

Mick Chambers and I visited Andrew Cunningham in his office to see if we could do any deals, but he refused. He was supporting a man called Giles Radice, who was head of the GMB research department, a nice man but hardly a Northerner. The miners had put in two nominations, Frank McKenna, from Birtley, and Gerald Herron, from Dunston. These nominations were all included on a short-list of five. The other candidates were myself and Bill Graham, from Sacriston, a representative of the National Union of Teachers.

The selection process took place at Birtley Parish Hall in 1972, and candidates were eliminated. Firstly Frank McKenna, then Gerald Herron. There was three of us left. I was eliminated as the third candidate and only Giles Radice, sponsored by the GMB, and Bill Graham, of the NUT, were left in the running.

My delegates decided, as part of a deal, to put their votes behind Giles Radice. So what started out as a campaign to stop the GMB getting the seat vacated due to the death of Norman Pentland, resulted in the T&G helping to secure the seat for Giles Radice.

When the election took place, the Labour majority went down from 22,000 to 7,000. Giles Radice became a very good constituency MP and we became very good friends.

Chapter Eighteen

My desire to see some form of regional government in the North of England to mitigate the years of high unemployment and economic deprivation took me into wide discussions with people both in the region and in Scotland in the three years after the election in Chester-le-Street. Many of the people to whom I spoke, shared my passion for devolution, not to see introduced just another tier of Government, but a regional assembly made up of some of the most astute political brains in the North, who knew the region's problems and how they could be best addressed, and would be given the powers to put things right.

My drive for regional government led me into discussions with many people, who shared the same belief and desire and who were motivated, like me, by the unfairness of the system, particularly in that gaping chasm which was and still is the North/South divide.

My election as chairman of the Tyne and Wear Labour Party gave me the opportunity to see how politicians from different councils could work together towards a common aim. In my view, the establishment of the Tyne and Wear County Council was a great success and it was the pure vindictiveness of the Prime Minister, Margaret Thatcher, to abolish the Greater London Council, and castrate Ken Livingstone in the process, that saw the demise of the Tyne & Wear County Council and all the other metropolitan authorities which had worked so hard for their regions.

A great deal of work had been carried out by the Tyne & Wear County Council within the area but I would have liked to see some of the initiatives spread to other parts of the North East. During the later days of the county council, some tribal views started to emerge, mainly because of the possibility of inward investment opportunities, and these my-back-yard, parochial views could be counter productive. There was and needed to be a strong desire to work together for the common good of the region.

The pressure on my work and all my activities with the Labour Party took its toll on my private life and my marriage broke down. I was given custody of the two boys, Aidan and Barry, which put yet more strain on my domestic situation.

During this period my good friend and colleague Mick Chambers, the Regional General Secretary at the time, died in office. General Secretary Jack Jones decided not to appoint a replacement immediately, preferring to transfer a regional secretary from Humberside, Dave Shenton, to the Newcastle office on a temporary basis. Dave Shenton only survived a few months. He, too, died in office.

Jack Jones decided the northern region needed some time to settle down in terms of its administration and transferred Moss Evans, the national organisational officer, into the region from his London office to oversee the work of the region for six months, in order that proper consideration could be given to appointing a new regional T&G secretary.

Prior to all this, the regional finance administrator Arthur Manners left the office, which was a serious blow, as he was in control of all the administration. However, we managed to find a replacement in Jim Smyth, from Ireland, who became involved in the membership side of the union and also became a good friend of mine.

Alan Dixon, another full-time official, was an energetic force in the office. Him and Jim Smith became good pals as well as their wives Audrey and Marie. They always like to get involved in the social activities arranged for the union members and their families and seeking various donations from employers for the prizes.

During 1974, I met and married Lirena. When I was left to bring up the two boys, Lirena used to help me out in the house. I proposed to her one night when we were having dinner and she accepted.

We had a November wedding and Giles Radice was best man. I had known Lirena when she worked as a receptionist in the regional office before she started her nursing training at Newcastle General Hospital. I had always thought of her as a nice, caring person. The wedding was a lovely family occasion, with all the parents and the rest of the families in attendance as well as Aidan and Barry. I was extremely fortunate I was able to meet Lirena because we had formed a partnership that has lasted for many years and has produced two lovely children, Lucy-Ann and Joanne.

It started to become clear during Moss Evans' six months within the region that he was seeking the views of leading activists about a successor to become Regional Secretary. He spoke to many members of the regional committee, as well as other leading lights within the union. I realised that Jack Jones had a particular style of leadership that he wanted in the rest of the country. Jack Jones had taken over from Frank Cousins in 1969, having previously been the Assistant General Secretary. However, before moving to London, he was the Regional Secretary in the Midlands and was very successful, greatly increasing the membership and presiding over some of the best agreements reached by unions and employers in the country. His view was that regional secretaries were general secretaries in their own right, in control of their own funds, staff and administration. His view on devolution and power were very well known. He was a decentralist who believed in the democratic control being within the regions. His style of leadership was to encourage members to be active within their union and to bring power on to the shop floor. Since he took over the leadership of the union in 1969, he had actively engaged politicians and governments to introduce rules and legislation to protect workers at work. He carried the national TUC with him in this direction and he managed to persuade the Callaghan Government in the 1970s to bring in the Employment Protection Act, The Trade Union and Labour Relations Act and the Health and Safety at Work legislation.

He was also actively involved in the setting up of the Advisory, Conciliation and Arbitration Service (ACAS).

The Conservative Party during its time in office in the 1970s thought Jack Jones had more power in the country than the Prime Minister.

As the General Secretary of the T&G, because of his own background and beliefs, he enhanced the roles of the 11 regional general secretaries. The regional secretaries became known as "regional barons" with almost unlimited power.

When seeking views of membership in the region, Moss Evans was trying to get someone in the mould of Jack Jones. When the job was advertised, I wasn't sure about applying, though Moss Evans did encourage me to do so. Applying would mean being interviewed by the General Executive Council in London. I thought long and hard about this decision and I thought if I did apply and was successful I could bring my own philosophy to the job, and hopefully do something to improve the regional economy. I also realised that if I got the job, I would have some influence within the Regional Labour Party. I also felt we should be enlarging the membership and increasing the amount of collective bargaining that was going on in many industries. At the time, this was totally unorganised.

I discussed my thoughts with Lirena, realising it would be a time consuming, stressful and demanding job. We also had our first daughter to consider, Joanne Louise was born to us on December 5th 1975.

While Lirena was in the maternity ward having Joanne, she missed out on a ceremony in Newcastle General Hospital where she was to receive the Silver Health Award as runner-up in her three-year nursing training course. However, her mother attended on her behalf to receive the award, which made us all very proud.

Lirena encouraged me to apply for the job and I completed the application form stating all of the qualifications I had within the organisation and outlining some of my views and philosophies. I was aware that many other senior officials within the union, who had a lot more service than myself, were also interested in the post. There was also a lot of views being expressed about who the successful candidate should be.

After a few weeks, all of the candidates were invited to London to be interviewed by the General Executive Council. I knew when I went to the interview that Jack Jones and the rest of the GEC were looking for someone who could provide a modern style of leadership and a new image. I also realised they wanted more political influence, not just in the regions but within the country. They wanted to bring about change from the old days to meeting the challenges of the future. They were also keen to involve membership more within the union agreements and also within the administration. This was, as I understood it, Jack Jones' vision.

During my interview, I spelt out quite clearly all of my views on these subjects. I felt we needed a more modern style, more political influence. I felt I was the man for the job who could achieve this. I thought I was pressing the right buttons. My only drawback was my age. I was 39 and the youngest candidate within the field.

I returned home, after giving my best at the interview, and awaited a call from Jack Jones. At about 10pm, the phone rang and I was gobsmacked when Jack Jones told me I had got the job as the secretary of the T&G in the northern region. I didn't really know what to say, but thanked him for the confidence that the GEC had placed in me.

The following morning, I went into the regional office and it became clear within an hour to everyone that I had been appointed the new Regional Secretary of the T&G; some of the other candidates around the head office had been told. I was personally delighted that I had now been given the opportunity by Britain's biggest trade union to head up its organisation in the North with all of the implications and responsibilities that went with it.

For the next few days I was on cloud nine, receiving letters and phone calls from many people. Many of the local politicians and heads of the unions within the region also rang me to congratulate me.

One of the first things I did when I became the Regional Secretary was to burn the chair that had been used by previous holders of the post. I felt that this was symbolic and I wanted to ensure that everything was started anew.

I had been in the post for no more than two or three weeks when I was told that my appointment as Regional Secretary had also been recognised by the regional TUC and that I was to be appointed by the regional TUC on to the Port of Tyne Authority as the representative from the trade union movement. This was something I neither expected nor considered but I did stay with the Port of Tyne Authority for 26 years from my appointment in 1976. I was also elected on to the regional TUC and the regional Labour Party.

In fact for the next few weeks I was the most sought after person within the regional trade union and Labour movement. This was nothing to do with my personal qualities; no one yet had been able to assess what my strengths or weakness were. It was all to do with the fact that I was now the head of Britain's largest union within the northern region and regional secretary of the second largest union within the North of England. The biggest was the GMB.

I realised now that I had arrived but considered one sound piece of advice imparted to me by Jack Jones. He said many, many, people, among them politicians, trade unionists and employers, will want me on the way up and will seek my advice, but when they have achieved their objectives they will ignore you. I found this has been the case right through my career in the trade unions, with one or two exceptions.

My elation at reaching the top of my union, at least in the northern region, lasted a long, long, time. I now had more influence than ever; influence that would extend to the northern regional Labour Party, and I would have the ear of big employers, future investors, future MPs and even future Government ministers.

My vision of a devolved North, free from the shackles of centralised power, appeared now at least a possibility, rather than a pipe-dream, if I could spread the message to those who needed to know, from the powerful positions I now held.

What I needed was to catch those people on the way up – those whom Jack Jones said might seek my advice. I hoped to catch them, and I hoped above hope, that they would listen.

Chapter Nineteen

The biggest task I faced within my first few months in office was to try to help save the jobs of 1,500 people employed by Brentford Nylons at its factories in Cramlington, Northumberland, and Felling, in Gateshead. The task would see me working behind the scenes in negotiations with a man Ted Heath described as "the unacceptable face of capitalism", the millionaire businessman, Tiny Rowland, the boss of international trading giant Lonrho.

Brentford Nylons was owned by two Armenian brothers and manufactured bedding made out of nylon. The company had received major grants from the Government to build a new factory in Cramlington and everything seemed to be going well. We had a shop steward there and recognition and it seemed like a successful operation. Out of the blue, without any notice, the two brothers decided to leave the company and left no one in charge to carry on the business. This shocked all the workers who had no inkling about what was happening.

The T&G decided to campaign with the Government to try to save the company and a number of meetings took place in London with various ministers. One day, Jack Jones rang me to say that there had been a meeting in London of the Industrial Development Board, which was a national organisation under the auspices of the DTI which examined inward investment proposals and grants to help industry provide work in areas of high unemployment. He said that he had spoken to someone from Lonrho who seemed to be interested in taking over the factory at Cramlington. The only problem was that Lonrho's chairman Tiny Rowland was known throughout the world for his views.

Rowland was involved in the Rhodesian political scene and was a very good friend of Ian Smith, who was trying to secure independence for Rhodesia. He had flown Smith back and forward to Mozambique for discussions. The reason why he had all that interest in that part of the world was because Lonrho had a lot of metal interests in both countries. When Jack Jones mentioned this to me I was a bit surprised, but said as far as I was concerned if the company was prepared to save all the jobs in the North East, I was prepared to give it some consideration and recommend it to the workers. Jack Jones told me that he had spoken to Lonrho representatives and had told them that the person who would need convincing in the northern region was Joe Mills, because of his influence in the unions and the Labour Party.

Two or three days later, my secretary Ruth Birbeck rang me to tell me there was a Mr Tiny Rowland on the phone wanting to speak to me about the Cramlington situation. Initially, I thought someone was setting me up, but the call was put through. He introduced himself and said his company was interested in taking over the Cramlington and Felling sites of Brentford Nylons but he wondered what reaction there would be from people in the North by proposing this. I said to him that as far as I was concerned his reputation both nationally and internationally had nothing to do with the situation. If he could find ways and means of securing Brentford Nylons into his own company to save all these jobs, then certainly I would co-operate as fully as I could. He thanked me and said he would contact me later on to speak to me about developments. He asked me for my home number, which I was surprised at. He said he wanted the proposal keeping secret until a final decision was made.

About two or three days later, I got another call from him

and he told me that Lonrho was actively considering the situation and was approaching the Government to see if there were any grants that could be made available, bearing in mind the Armenian brothers who had the Brentford Nylons factory in Cramlington had already received substantial grants.

After this conversation, I had a number of chats with Tiny Rowland about the way this development would take place. It was rather odd at the time because I was speaking to people in the regional trade unions and the Labour Party about a number of issues, including the unacceptable face of capitalism. Tiny Rowland and the way he was operating in Africa was mentioned, but I was sworn to secrecy about the potential North East deal. I thought that if these people knew that I was having these lengthy conversations with Tiny Rowland at the time, they would have fallen from their chairs.

One night at home, Tiny Rowland rang me to say he was now at the HQ in London and his board had decided to proceed with the takeover of Brentford Nylons. He asked me to help him to announce this at a Press conference to people in the North. I suggested to him we should have a Press conference, preferably at my office, in order that people could see that the union was endorsing this move to save the jobs. I also said it could be politically sensitive and suggested that I should be involved in the Press conference to answer any questions in this regard. He supported this and suggested the Press conference should be held the following day. He said he would send up Lonrho directors Edward Du Can and Dr Kalil Osman, a Sudanese sheik with about 30 per cent shares in the company. I was taken aback when he suggested he had the power to send these two people to the North and it demonstrated quite clearly the way he operated.

I hastily rang a number of people in order to set up the Press conference at 11am on the Monday but gave them no details, other than to tell them we had saved the jobs of the workers at Brentford Nylons. After I had finished all the conversations on the phone I decided to go to my local pub with my wife Lirena for a drink, as I normally did on a Sunday night.

In the bar we stood talking to one or two of the locals, parish and district councillors, putting the world to rights. During the conversation one of the them mentioned a programme that had been on television that evening called "The Unacceptable Face of Capitalism - The Mozambique Connection", featuring Tiny Rowland.

"Wasn't that the man who rang you at home tonight?" my wife asked, innocently. I burst out laughing and said Tiny Rowland was hardly the type of person to ring me about anything. I had nothing in common with him. Lirena looked at me rather quizzically and everyone shared in the joke.

It wasn't until we were walking home that I confessed to Lirena that it was the same Tiny Rowland who had rang me at home, but I had hardly dare mention it in the pub as I was sworn to secrecy until the Press conference the following day.

The Press conference went ahead as expected. I went to Newcastle Airport to meet Kalil Osman and Edward Du Can who had flown in on a private jet used by the Lonrho company.

At the Press conference I told the assembled media that Lonrho had decided to take over Brentford Nylons and safeguard all the jobs. This was brilliant news for the North. I was asked a lot of questions about Lonrho, but made the point that, as far as I was concerned, Lonrho's business elsewhere was its own concern. It had come to the North to save the jobs of 1,500 people and we could guarantee its investment would be justified.

I thought that would be the end of my conversations with Tiny Rowland, but he called me once during the steel strikes to say his works in Sheffield was being picketed by the steelworkers' union and he asked if I could I do anything to help him. I was rather surprised and told him the Yorkshire region had nothing to do with me but he could ring my colleague Mike Davey and see what, if anything, Mike could do. He did call Mike, who told him he could not help.

I was later contacted by the managing director of the Lonrho group on behalf of Tiny Rowland, asking if I could send a letter to Tiny Rowland, indicating that the terms and conditions of employment at Cramlington were very good. I asked why he wanted this letter and he said the company was having discussions about the takeover of the Harrods Group and he wanted to ensure that the unions involved realised that Lonrho had a good track record for industrial relations in the country and wanted to quote Lonrho textiles – now the company name – as an example. I said I couldn't do this, as it would mean entering an activity that was very sensitive at the time.

Clearly, the Lonrho group was trying to use me in its bid to influence the unions in its take-over bid of Harrods.

Later on, at conferences I attended with the Labour Party or the TUC, several people referred to me sarcastically as Tiny Rowland's mate.

My dealings with Tiny Rowland surprised a few people within the T&G, as he was an anathema to everything they stood for.

It wasn't the last time I would surprise people within the union movement.

In 1977 I had to ensure that we took our delegation to the T&G's biennial delegate conference on the Isle of Man. Getting 200 people from the North East to the Isle of Man at virtually the same time for this important conference, with some travelling by rail, cars, mini buses or chartered coaches, could prove to be a logistical nightmare. So I decided we would fly. We chartered a plane from Newcastle. This caused some mirth around the Northern region as it had never been done before. It was seen as a bit of a flash idea. When I mentioned it to Jack Jones he burst out laughing.

I was aware that many of the delegates had never flown before, including my mother-in-law Amy, who was travelling with us to look after Joanne during the conference.

We left Newcastle Airport in the morning and arrived at the Isle of Man within an hour. All of the delegates enjoyed the trip. It was the talk of the conference that the Northern region of the T&G had arrived by aeroplane. It was quite a coup, as far as I was concerned, and gave us the right image and profile at the conference.

After the Isle of Man conference, I received a letter from the Lord Lieutenancy in Durham enclosing two tickets to a celebratory service in Durham Cathedral for the Silver Jubilee year, and I was told that there would be quite a lot of people attending involved in the Jubilee activities. I had been given a position on a committee overseeing the distribution of funds for Jubilee celebrations, just before our Isle of Man conference.

I looked in my diary and realised I was in London on business on the day of the service, so I decided to give the tickets to my parents. I was sure they would enjoy the event.

When I returned from London, I rang my mother and father to ask them how they had enjoyed the celebratory service in Durham Cathedral. They told me a story that both amused me and almost filled me with horror.

My parents were queuing to go into the cathedral when one of the chaplains, who spotted the VIP-type tickets they were holding, ushered them to the front of the queue. They were taken into the cathedral and saw another cleric who took them to a front row. My parents couldn't understand why they had been given this privileged position, and were very nervous sitting there.

Shortly afterwards, another of the clerics ushered my mother and father to the centre of the aisle and asked them to stand there until the ceremony began. My father looked up the aisles and noticed there was about five other couples in a similar position, standing in the aisle just outside their seats.

The organ started up and then entered the Queen and Prince Philip, with their entourage. At this stage, my mother thought she and my father had been put in the wrong seats, and felt terribly embarrassed

The Queen and Prince Philip were introduced to the couples as they made their way slowly down the aisle and eventually, after much anxiety felt by my parents, reached where they were standing.

One of the clerics then said: "Your Majesty, may I introduce Mr Joe Mills and his wife." He went on to explain that Mr Joe Mills was a member of the Silver Jubilee committee and a senior member of the Transport and General Workers' Union. At this stage, my mother immediately said that my father wasn't Joe Mills, he was Larry Mills, and that she was my mother. Joe could not attend, my mother explained, because he had a bad chest and had asked his parents to deputise in his absence. My father noticed the look of surprise on the entourage and on the faces of the Queen and the Prince but the Queen was quick to react and said it was nice of me to ask my parents to attend on my behalf. Prince Philip commented on my father's DLI regimental tie, and they chatted about the regiment. They then left the my parents and continued with the ceremony and my parents went back to their seats.

When I heard this story from my mother and father I didn't know what to think. I hadn't any idea at all that they were to be presented to the Queen. If I had known I would have sent my apologies to the organising committee. When I told my colleagues the excuse my mother had given for my non attendance, they suggested I should go around coughing for a few days, otherwise people might suggest I had snubbed the Queen.

Chapter Twenty

The case for the North, which spelt out clearly the need for local authorities, trade unions, employers and other organisations to work together and speak with one voice to Government, was formalised in 1978 with the production of a Labour Party policy document "Let's Pull Together for a Better North".

The Prime Minister, James Callaghan, agreed to meet a delegation from the North at 10 Downing Street, where we would be able to present the document and speak freely about why we believed the North needed to be treated as a special case.

Unemployment was still unacceptable high in the region and economic deprivation as widespread as ever. Representatives from the T&G had attended numerous meetings with the TUC and the Labour Party to try to address the issues. Representations had been made to several Government ministers but we seemed to be making no headway at all. Jobs were being lost at a substantial rate and while initiatives were taken to bring more jobs and inward investment to the region, the net result was that we were losing jobs at a fairly rapid rate. Once again, the question of working together in a co-ordinated way seemed to be the best way forward.

Paul Nicholson, who owned Vaux Breweries in Sunderland, was the chairman of the regional CBI at the time and he endorsed and supported this co-ordinated approach – against the view of the Tory Party.

Jack Dormand, the MP for Easington, now Lord Dormand, arranged the meeting with the Prime Minister and some of his ministers in the autumn of 1978. We were delighted to be taking our case to the heart of Government.

There was a delegation of ten – five from the TUC and five from the Labour Party. Before we went into the meeting, it was agreed that the chairman of the TUC, George Arnold, a full-time official of the AEEW, would speak on behalf of the TUC and that I would speak on behalf of the Regional Labour Party.

Walking through the doors of Number 10, we were ushered into the Cabinet Room, to be sat opposite the PM and some of his ministers. James Callaghan said he was delighted to invite us to present our case.

Both George Arnold and I then went through our arguments about the need for the Government to create some unified body within the North of England to represent the collective problems that we had, and the document – Let's Pull Together for a Better North – identified the structures that would allow this to happen.

We were questioned at length about the arguments and ideas we put forward during the hour-long meeting. Most of the delegates began putting their own arguments forward – which went against the discipline we had expected and the strategy we had agreed. In fact, after the meeting, the only person who hadn't given his views was Sam Scott, the General Secretary of the NUM. James Callaghan recognised this and before the meeting ended said everyone seemed to have had their say apart from Sam Scott, whom he turned to and asked if he wanted to make a point.

Sam replied: "No, Prime Minister. We had an agreement before we came into this meeting that only George Arnold and Joe Mills would speak. As far as I am concerned, I am keeping my word, not like the rest of them." This brought a smile across the PM's face, and those of his ministers. At the end of the meeting, he said he would ask various ministers to investigate some of the arguments and points that had been raised in the document and report back to the Departments of State.

What was disappointing was that some weeks later we were advised that, having carried out the necessary consultation, the Government was of the view that there wasn't a great deal of enthusiasm in the North for the type of body proposed within the document. It would seem, we were told, that the Government wanted to pursue its objectives on its own and didn't want to come together in some kind of grand council, which would have meant bringing together trades unions, employers and local authorities and other groups.

This was a tremendous setback for the Northern region as far as we were concerned, and we realised we had a big and difficult task on our hands to try to get people to work together to deal with the serious problems of unemployment and economic deprivation. We wanted the type of spirit that existed in Scotland and in Wales. It would seem that this spirit had not yet emerged.

By the late 1970s, the T&GWU had a membership in excess of two million. The past five years had been a tremendous growth period, but the increase in membership was mainly due to many amalgamations and mergers. In fact, by 1978 there had been 82 to 84 mergers or amalgamations since the union was formed in 1922. One of the most important mergers happened in the late 60s-early 70s with the Scottish Commercial Morton's Union – The Scottish Transport Union – whose leader was Alex Kitson, a man well known in Labour circles throughout Great Britain. Some people were very critical of Alex because he had very close connections with Russia and some of the senior members of the Politburo. He was also a regular attender at various conferences in Russia, and during the Cold War he was frowned upon by the Government because of these visits.

Jack Jones felt the merger with the Scottish union was ideal for the T&G because it would bring together those who worked in transport on both sides of the border. Part of the deal for Alex, whose executive agreed, was that he would be given the position of executive officer and, consequently, became the union's representative on the Labour Party's National Executive, the top committee within the Labour Party.

In later years, Alex Kitson played a major part in the politics of the union and the wider Labour movement. He was a very likeable character, who was born and bred in Glasgow and had come up very much the hard way. He worked in his early days as a milkman and was very friendly with Sean Connery.

In 1978, Jack Jones retired as the General Secretary of the T&G, and everyone realised he would be a tremendous miss. He had taken the union to more than two million members and had made a great deal of progress when he was member of the general executive council of the TUC in discussions with the Government.

Moss Evans succeeded Jack Jones in 1978 and he told me that everyone would point the finger and say he was no Jack Jones. But he recalled that many had said in the past that Jack Jones was no Frank Cousins. Like Jack Jones, he established his trade union credentials in the Midlands and was a very successful official before moving to London as a national organiser. His stance against Jim Callaghan, against the pay policies within the unions in 1979, led to weeks of strike action and some say helped to secure a Tory Government. Moss Evans was only reflecting the policies of the T&G formed during its 1979 biennial delegate conference, which was to secure increased terms and conditions of employment by free collective bargaining and entering into no deals with the Government. He suffered a personal tragedy during his time in office when his son Kevin was killed in a car crash.

Campaigning for the general secretaryship of Britain's largest union was very stressful for all concerned, particularly the candidates. When Moss Evans was declared the winner, I invited him to the North for a couple of days' holiday, before taking up his post as Britain's most powerful union leader.

He spent a day by the river at Annitsford, Consett, with Laura, his wife, Lirena and I and our baby daughter Joanne, before we accompanied him to the Post House Hotel in Washington, where he was staying. After we dropped him off, we agreed to pick him up after a couple of hours to go to Newcastle for dinner. I was to collect Lirena's mother Amy from Newcastle so she could babysit for us. When I returned home with Amy, I noticed Moss's car outside our house and presumed he had misunderstood the arrangements. However, when I entered our house Moss and Laura were inside with drinks in their hands looking rather flustered. Moss told me that when he came down from his room at the hotel to have a drink at the bar he noticed a large crowd gathering outside the main entrance. On closer examination he realised it was a T&G picket line from Leeds, trying to pressurise Trust House Forte, the owners of the Washington Moat House Hotel, to recognise the T&G. The picket line was part of a national campaign.

I hadn't realised this was going on, otherwise I would not have booked Moss Evans into this particular hotel. He also was unaware of the campaign as this had not been his responsibility until his recent appointment as General Secretary. I couldn't believe the situation I had got him into. I was interested to know how he had got out of the hotel unseen by the pickets. His picture had been all over the papers the previous weeks during the election for the General Secretary. Moss burst out laughing and told me he had removed his glasses, combed his hair forward, turned up his coat collar and linked Laura, walking unsteadily passed the pickets, giving the impression he was an elderly gentleman. One of the pickets had actually helped him down the step! Fortunately, there were no pickets when we returned after dinner and this incident was a secret between us for many years.

Moss had a long serious illness which allowed a vacuum in the leadership to be filled by various political interest groups. While

Moss was away from work, Alex Kitson assumed the role of the General Secretary for more than six months. Moss Evans' absence was greatly missed by the union because it needed some stability.

In his autobiography of 1986, Jack Jones did not devote a single line to Moss Evans, which seemed to suggest to union observers his disapproval of his stewardship of the union. However, I always found Moss Evans a very pleasant and likeable individual. Although he had a reputation to be able to speak for long periods, he was quite amusing.

Shortly after his election as General Secretary, I was asked by Moss to attend a conference in Cyprus. It would seem that the World Federation of Free Trades Unions, which was a very left-wing-dominated congress of unions, was meeting in Nicosia to look at the future of Cyprus because of the divisions that already existed between the Turkish and the Greek Cypriots. The Turks had invaded the Island in 1974 and after a lot of fighting, the United Nations was able to broker a ceasefire. The island was virtually split in two. Cyprus itself was of strategic importance to the world because of its position and everyone was interested in seeing how the voting would turn out.

The British TUC did not want to send anyone to the conference because it was not affiliated to the World Federation of Free Trades Unions due to its left wing dominance. However, Moss Evans was keen, along with the GEC of our union, to find out what was going on at the conference and he asked me to attend in a low key capacity and report back later.

About three days later, Alex Kitson rang me to say that I should go to the Foreign Office to receive a full briefing about the current situation in Cyprus so it could arrange for me to visit the leaders and politicians within the Greek sector and also a minister in the Turkish sector, a leading politician. I went to the Foreign Office.

I was later approached by Ken Gill, the General Secretary of the Draughtsmen and Allied Technicians' Union, who was also Chairman of the Union Travel organisation which arranged trips abroad for trade union members. It was a holiday company registered with the TUC. He wanted me to visit various hotels in the Greek sector to see if they were suitable for members to visit.

I was a bit confused at this stage. I was asked by Moss to attend the conference as an observer. I was also now on a job for the Foreign Office and Ken Gill asked me to look at some hotels on the Greek side of the island, while I was there.

As the conference proceeded, I got the distinct impression that the speakers were more interested in the strategic importance of Cyprus in relation to their own countries, rather than concerned about the people of Cyprus themselves. As this went on, I became more and more concerned about the whole event.

After lunch, I raised my hand to speak and was invited on to the rostrum. So much for my low-key observing role!

I said I felt the conference was missing the whole point of the Cyprus question. It had not mentioned the people on the island. I went on at length about this and I received good applause when I finished. As I left the rostrum I was approached by a number of journalists from Cyprus who asked me for my comments further. I realised at this stage that I was getting into deep water because I wasn't supposed to be making any contributions.

That evening on the local television my speech was referred to and the fact that I was from the T&G in Great Britain. I was now quite concerned.

After the conference, and some time looking at hotels, as I had agreed, I returned to England and rang Moss Evans about my trip. He said he had already had a fairly comprehensive report sent to him, I didn't know who it was from.

What I had expected to be a fairly quiet trip to Cyprus as an observer to find out what was going on turned out to be fairly exciting, full of intrigue and sometimes very stressful.

I couldn't help but have my say at the conference, even though I was under orders to observe only. Perhaps the sight of the hundreds of delegates in the crowd brought out the showman in me.

Chapter Twenty One

During 1978, I was becoming more conscious that the trade union movement and the Callaghan government were not seeing eye to eye. The question of free collective bargaining and all of its ramifications was causing concern to the cabinet. While the policy of the T&G was quite clear in this regard and our members were encouraged to pursue these policies, the Government wanted some form of wage accord with the TUC in order to stabilise the economy.

I became more and more concerned that we had returned a Labour Government in 1974 and, within a few years, we seemed to be on a collision course. We had achieved a number of things for the protection of workers from the Labour Government, such as the Trade Unions and Labour Relations Act, the Employment Protection Act, the Health and Safety at Work Act and also the establishment of ACAS, which had to regulate the relationship between employers and the trade unions.

Although there was still problems in relation to equal pay and low wages in many industries, I had reservations about the whole question of unfettered free collective bargaining. It would seem to me that the strongest would always prevail and the weakest would be left at the post.

At the Labour Party conferences in 1977 and 1978, when I was attending as a delegate from the T&G, our block vote was in excess of two million members, all supporting the line which, quite clearly, the Government didn't want. Nevertheless, that was the policy of the T&G as agreed at its biennial delegate conference. I felt uneasy that we appeared to be moving into a crisis situation and could possibly lose the Labour Government.

I was aware of this because of my involvement in the Labour Party in the northern region and did not have the centre left type philosophies that seemed to prevail in other parts of the movement in the country. There was some notable exceptions, mainly in the public sector, where the unions were quite rightly trying to improve their terms and conditions. The wages of public sector workers were on the low side and they had not been dealt with in a positive way. But the local authority employers were claiming they were paying as much as they could afford and it was up to the Government to allocate more resources in their direction.

To me, as an observer, the situation appeared to be a little crazy and I couldn't understand why the trade union movement and the Government could not come to some agreement.

As widely expected in 1979, prior to the General Election, things did get out of hand. It was the Winter of Discontent and the general public voted with its feet and refused to return a Labour Government.

This caused me a great deal of concern because I was still very conscious of the fact that here in the North we still had high unemployment, economic deprivation and all of the associated problems.

Another thing that was causing me some personal concern was that as principal officer with the T&G in the North, I wasn't convinced that the left-led executive of our union was pursuing the right policies that would ultimately bring about prosperity for the country, and in particular the North.

As expected, when the Labour Party lost the General Election, James Callaghan decided to stand down as Leader and the search for a new Labour Party leader started in earnest. A number of names were suggested as potentially good candidates from the various wings of the Labour Party, but there was no general consensus. Michael Foot , a good orator with well known left wing views, and who was very well known in the Labour Party, was seen to be the choice of many of the union's general secretaries, as well as certain people within the Labour Party. But there were other potential candidates suggested, who were not as extreme in their views as Michael Foot. The mood of the country at the time wouldn't seem to support a left-thinking candidate.

In order to persuade Michael Foot to stand as a candidate for the leadership, as he was initially reluctant to do so, many of us were encouraged to write to him asking him to stand. He stood and he was elected at the Labour Party conference as the new leader. The position of Deputy Leader also had to be filled and a lot of candidates were proposed. I took the view that I thought the best candidate for the deputy's post, to help mitigate against Michael Foot's left wing philosophies, should be Dennis Healey, and I campaigned within the Northern region, both within the trade union movement and within the Labour Party, on his behalf. Other candidates in the race included Tony Benn and John Silkin. Dennis Healey struck home by the narrowest of margins and became Deputy Leader of the Labour Party.

My involvement in Dennis Healey's campaign wasn't public knowledge until Dennis wrote his autobiography and revealed that the principal officer of the T&G was acting as his campaign manager in the North, when his own union was supporting either John Silkin or Tony Benn. Had this been known at the time, I am sure something would have been said by members of the T&G's General Executive Council and others.

One of the highlights of 1979 for me, personally, was on September 4th when Lirena gave birth to our second daughter, Lucy-Ann, at the Queen Elizabeth Hospital in Gateshead. I would have normally been attending the TUC conference during the first week in September but, this time, I was delighted to miss it.

1980 was a fairly eventful year. I was appointed by the union on to the commission of inquiry into the Labour Party, which had decided after the 1979 election defeat that it needed to examine the way it operated as a national organisation. The terms of reference were to look at the organisation of the party and how finance was raised and distributed. We decided to split the commission into two, one group to look at the finance and the other the organisation. I ended up on the organisational committee alongside Moss Evans, Dennis Healey, Joe Ashton, Eric Heffer, and other notables within the Labour and Trade Union movement. I enjoyed my 12 months on the commission because we were able to take evidence from various people within the party at all levels. It also gave me a tremendous insight into the organisation, how it was operating and how it should operate in the future.

In 1980, I was also elected chairman of the Northern Regional Labour Party – a job which I had been hankering after for a number of years since being appointed as the regional secretary of the T&G in 1976. I wanted to be able to use this position to try to ensure that the region once again spoke with one voice. I was terribly disappointed after we met Jim Callaghan in 1979 to be told that the region's various players were not prepared to work in a co-ordinated fashion – despite the "better North" campaign.

I thought his issue needed to be addressed in a very positive way and I intended to use my position on the Regional Labour Party to put forward the arguments for better co-operation and more collaboration between all the interested groups within the region, in order to try and address the severe problems we had seen over the years.

Early in 1981, I found myself spending some weeks in America on a study tour. This came about through a conversation I had with the American ambassador at the 1980 Durham Miners' Gala. The ambassador was invited every year by the miners. I was critical of some aspects of life in America, which prompted him to ask me if I had ever visited the United States. I said I hadn't, and he suggested I should.

A few weeks later I received a letter from the American Embassy in London inviting me to take part in a visitors' programme. I was told I would have to go on my own. I was very excited by the prospect but concerned I would be away from my family for so long. However, Lirena convinced me that it would be the chance of a lifetime, so I decided to accept.

My visit took me to Washington DC, to look at the political and trade union organisations I also visited many other areas of the United States, such as Atlanta, San Francisco, Chicago, Milwaukee and New York. It was a fascinating trip.

When I returned to Britain, I wrote to the American ambassador in London thanking him very much for the opportunity to visit his country, but commented that there was still a lot to put right in the United States.

I was pleased to get home, having missed my wife and daughters. I was keen to find out what had been going on on the political scene while I had been away, and endeavoured to find out. A great deal was starting to happen within the Regional Labour Party on the devolution issue. Calls were being made for some kind of development agency and some form of regional government. People realised that the election defeat of 1979 which brought the Tories to power would do nothing for the economy in the North East.

The Prime Minister, Margaret Thatcher, had made it clear to everyone that she intended an all-out attack on the major nationalised industries, such as coal and steel, which would have a devastating effect in the North. She intended to pursue a policy of privatisation right across the economy, sweeping away the nationalised industries and many of the public bodies supported by government in the past.

In order to enhance the case for regional devolution, a major conference was arranged to take place in Newcastle. Michael Foot was invited along as the main speaker.. His speech was well received, despite the fact that only an hour earlier I had to give him precise details of our plans and explain how we wanted devolved power to work. When I heard his speech afterwards I couldn't help but think he had a photographic memory. He dealt with every point in detail.

At the end of the conference, I felt we were now on our way, because we had the leader of the Labour Party on our side. But we still had a lot to do to convince our local authorities that this was the way forward for the northern region.

The Regional Labour Party then decided to hold a special conference in Darlington a few weeks later and invited representatives from local authorities to hear the arguments about the benefits of a closer working relationship with industry, trade unions and other bodies for inward investment opportunities and economic development.

I suggested we should invite Donald Dewar, the shadow secretary for Scotland, to address us because of his close ties with devolution and he agreed. The conference was a huge success as far as the Labour Party's northern regional executive was concerned, but there was still some unease among local authority leaders, particularly in Durham.

Within the next few weeks, members of the executive had to visit many Labour groups within the region to reinforce our message. It was from these initiatives that the Northern Regional Council Association was formed, introducing a closer working relationship between local authorities across the region and across political parties. It went on to play a major role in the creation of the Northern Development Company, which became the top job-seeking agency in Europe.

The board of the Northern Development Company (NDC) was made up of representatives from local authorities, trade unions, and the CBI. I was a member of the NDC at its inception and worked closely with others with one aim in mind, to improve the economy of the northern region.

At the same time, the Regional Labour Party held meetings with its counterparts in the North West and Yorkshire to enhance the case for regional devolution. The meetings were held in Wetherby and it became known as the Wetherby Group. Several members of the shadow cabinet used to attend these meetings, including John Prescott, who went on to become Deputy Prime Minister. The whole objective of the meeting was to get the issue of devolution into the next Labour Party manifesto, realising this was a difficult proposition.

In 1981, Lirena and I and the two girls, Lucy and Joanne, moved to Picktree Lodge, which was only 200 yards from our house in Birtley, into the Chester-le-Street District Council area.

At about the same time, I was appointed to the BBC Trade and Industry Consultative group. Moss Evans had decided to appoint me to this body from the TUC. Moss Evans, as a member of the General Executive Council of the TUC, was also chairman of the media committee and felt it was a good idea if a principal T&G officer had some involvement with the BBC at national level in trade and industry matters. This was a very influential position and I was able to make a contribution to the debates on how the BBC was treating the industry and trade matters in its television programmes.

Shortly after my appointment, I was approached by Paul Nicholson, the chairman of Sunderland's Vaux Brewery, who told met he was developing a consortium to make a bid for Tyne Tees Television. The company was part of the Trident Group, the same as Yorkshire Television, and a number of people in the North, particularly within the business community, felt Tyne Tees should be an independent organisation.

I had to consult with Moss Evans to see whether or not I could be part of this group.

The group of members included Dennis Stephenson, the chairman of the Aycliffe and Peterlee Development Corporation and Sir Richard Storey, the chairman of Portsmouth and Sunderland Newspapers. There was also a wider support group, which included Sir Tom Cowie, who was then chairman of Sunderland Football Club, and Denise Roberston, a well-known broadcaster.

Moss Evans agreed I should be involved with the group and also agreed to make a substantial contribution to pursue the bid process. This put me in a completely different environment to the one I was used to; sitting with a number of North East industrial giants trying to bid for a television station very well-known and popular in the region. The idea of the bid was to put alternative proposals to broadcast in the northern region and part of Yorkshire. My part of the process was to talk about the community involvement and what people would expect from the broadcasting station, and also to talk about the industrial relations side of the business. The whole process took almost one year. I was involved in meetings across the country, including in Fleet Street, talking to potential advertisers and newspaper owners and publishers.

Just before the presentation of our case to the Independent Broadcasting Authority at its headquarters in London, we held a meeting to determine our approach. Paul Nicholson was to deal with the whole financial structure, Richard Storey was to deal with the wider implications for the media, Dennis Stephenson would be presenting arguments on behalf of the public sector, and I would be dealing with the industrial relations package.

Part of my plan was to argue that rather than unions within Tyne Tees being part of the national bargaining structure, that we should have a planned bargaining arrangement or a local agreement for all workers so they could negotiate directly with their employer. This was fairly revolutionary at the time in broadcasting, but I knew I was on safe ground because this was a policy that my own union was pursuing.

When we met the IBA, the meeting lasted more than two hours and I thought we had presented a positive case. However, some weeks later we were advised that our application had not been successful and Trident still maintained ownership of Tyne Tees Television. But it was instructed to give more authority to the local directors of both Yorkshire and TTTV.

Consequently Dennis Stephenson was asked to join the Tyne Tees board as was Paul Nicholson. Richard Storey was also approached to become a director but declined.

I wasn't given any opportunity at all. Clearly, they did not want a trade unionist on the board of Tyne Tees, which I suppose would have been a radical move had it come around.

Chapter Twenty Two

A barrister, and T&G member, by the name of Tony Blair, visited me at my office in Newcastle in late 1982, and told me he was interested in standing as a candidate for Labour in the safe seat of Sedgefield in County Durham. He had joined the union at our head office branch in London He said he had lived in Shincliffe, County Durham, as a boy, which gave him something of a Northern profile.

We had a long conversation and I was impressed with his honesty, his vision and his far-reaching views, many of which I shared. He was keen to see the Labour Party modernise, and to see it working more closely with industry to improve the economic performance of the Northern region and of the rest of the country. In fact, many of his ideas were those that my own union was trying to pursue in the North East, although not totally in accord with those of the T&G's General Executive Council.

At the time, everyone was anticipating a General Election in 1983 and this caused a flurry of activity among a lot of would-be parliamentarians, who were looking to secure nominations for seats across the country. Many MPs were also expected to stand down.

I was not convinced at this stage, by any means, that we were heading for a 1983 Labour victory, because, since 1979, I had not seen any real improvements.

All of the Labour Party and TUC conferences since 1979 had been full of conflict and I think Michael Foot, continuing to argue his case from a very left wing viewpoint, wasn't encouraging the people in the country to vote for him.

I knew from a personal point of view from the people I met and chatted with, that there was a great deal of disillusionment within both the trade union and Labour movements, at least in the North of England.

A lot of people were not aware of the influence trade unions had in the selection of people to stand for parliament. During 1982, and in subsequent years, I had numerous would-be parliamentarians visiting my office and my home asking for the T&G's support in selection conferences.

The trade unions influenced the selection process in two ways; firstly the T&G always encouraged its branches to affiliate to the local Labour Party, which would allow them to send delegates to selection conferences. The more branches affiliated to the constituency, the more delegates they had and the bigger the influence. Secondly, the unions' national executives would interview people interested in becoming MPs, and if they shared the union's point of view, they would be placed on what was commonly known as the A list. Therefore, people who were on these A lists had to pursue the policies of the trade union which sponsored them. As the GEC of the T&G had left wing policies, it naturally followed that the people on the A list, sponsored by the T&G, had left wing opinions.

In late 1982, I was advised that a former government minister under James Callaghan was wanting to be considered for the Sedgefield constituency. His name was Les Huckfield. This man had extremely left wing views and had the support of various left-wing factions within the unions and of other left-wing groups throughout the country.

My union did not have many delegates to the Sedgefield Constituency Labour Party, but I realised that it had become common knowledge that Les Huckfield was on the T&G A list and supported by the union. It was thought that some of the other unions without candidates might, out of loyalty, support Les Huckfield. This problem exercised my mind for a number of days.

As regional Labour Party chairman, I took the view that Les Huckfield would be bad news for the North. Some days later Les Huckfield appeared in my office with a man named Alan Meale, a research officer with the rail union Aslef, who later became an MP. Les Huckfield told me he was going to visit a number of the Sedgefield constituency delegates to try and persuade them to vote for him, and he wanted a letter of introduction from me to advise people he was supported by the T&G and was a member of the A list. He also asked me to give him a personal recommendation.

I told him that I was obliged as a principal officer to tell people he was on the A list, which was a matter of fact, but I was not prepared to give him my personal support. He was taken aback by this response and we had some heated words. He said I was ignoring the wishes of the union's General Executive Council and he said that I was totally out of order. I dictated an open letter to my secretary indicating that he was an A list candidate and nothing more. I signed the letter and passed it to him. He left the office with Alan Meale following, very annoyed.

It was only a few days later that Tony Blair turned up at my office. After our discussion, and reflecting on the visit I had from Les Huckfield and Alan Meale only about a week earlier, the young Tony blair appeared like a breath of fresh air. I told him I thought we could support his candidature because he was a member of our union, and I would be prepared to do so. I explained that we did not have many delegates in Sedgefield, but we had many friends in the North and supporters in other unions whom I would try to influence. I would try and seek their support for him. When he left my office, I asked Tony Blair to keep in touch.

I then contacted one of the T&G officials in Stockton, Gordon McClean, told him about the conversation I had had with

Tony Blair and about my dilemma with Les Huckfield. I told him that I had decided to personally support Tony Blair and to ignore the T&G General Executive Council's recommendation. I asked Gordon McClean to spend some time in Sedgefield, where we had some members in different factories, and to promote Tony Blair where he could among the other unions. I also asked him to ensure that any suggestion that the T&G was supporting Les Huckfield should be ignored.

He seemed a little nervous about this, because of the GEC's position, but I said I would send my instructions to him in writing, to protect him from any flack. For the next few days, Gordon visited many people on our behalf, making sure that people knew that Les Huckfield was not the preferred candidate as far as the T&G's northern regional office was concerned, but that he was on the A list as a preferred candidate supported by the national union. I did likewise with my trade union and local authority colleagues. Over the next few weeks, I received a number of abusive telephone calls from across the country.

The rest, of course, is history. Tony Blair got the selection nomination and went on to become the Member of Parliament for Sedgefield, and on to better things.

One of the seats in the northern region that was causing the Labour party some concern was Redcar. The sitting candidate, James Tinn, kept threatening to leave the House of Commons and wasn't too sure if he would stand for the next Parliament. However, we had gone through the process for the whole of the northern region and thought James Tinn had decided to continue. One day, though, Bert Twigg, the regional organiser of the Labour Party contacted me to say that James Tinn had decided to resign, only three or four weeks before the General Election, giving us no time at all to select candidates in the normal way.

I received a telephone call from Neil Kinnock, telling us we had to draw up a short-list of four in order to ensure we met the deadline for the election. Bert Twigg and I got together to draw up a list of four people. We came up with three. We realised we needed to have a fourth person, and decided that one of the best people to fill the fourth slot was Mo Mowlam, who had been put in second place for the Tyne Bridge constituency behind David Clelland. Mo was a very likeable person and very much a political activist. We decided to put her name on a short-list of four for the selection conference which was hastily called in Redcar.

I rang Mo Mowlam and told her what we had done. She was absolutely overjoyed and expressed herself in typical Mo Mowlam fashion. Mo went to the selection conference and received the overwhelming support of the delegates to become the candidate for the constituency at the 1983 General Election.

Mo rang me that night, along with Hilary Armstrong, after the selection conference. She had obviously been celebrating securing the nomination. Redcar was a difficult constituency with various factions, some believe it or not, religious. During the election campaign Mo went in to all the hostels and the community centres and, in her own inimitable way, was able to bring all the people together for a successful General Election result. I often think about Mo and her exploits in Northern Ireland as a very successful minister of state. When she was given this position by Tony Blair, I often thought that if anyone could bring the factions together it was Mo Mowlam. My colleagues within the T&G felt the same way.

The day after Tony Blair's selection in Sedgefield, I received a phone call from Alex Kitson, who told me that some of the executive was going ballistic at my refusal to support Les Huckfield as the A list candidate and my active support for Tony Blair. The verbal abuse directed at me among my T&G national colleagues, I was aware, went on for a number of years, particularly when Tony Blair became a shadow spokesman and was promoting policies that the T&G's national executive did not like. This was a rather uncomfortable period for me but I knew that the type of policies that Tony Blair was pursuing as an individual, I believed, would ultimately prevail in the Labour Party in general and could be the type of policy that the country would support rather than the dated views constantly pursued by my left-wing General Executive Council and other organisations of a similar persuasion.

After Tony Blair was elected as a Member of Parliament, he spent a lot of time in the Commons and, I imagined, was a little disappointed that he was still just a member of the opposition. But he also spent a lot of time at various weekend schools, which I organised, talking to my shop stewards and union representatives. This helped to convince my colleagues who weren't already, that they should become members of the Labour Party.

Tony Blair also visited my home in Picktree Lodge in Chester-le-Street to have discussions on a number of matters relating to politics and trade unionism. I was also able to introduce him to some other influential people within the region with whom I had dealings with in industrial relations.

Just before the 1987 General Election, my regional committee of the T&G interviewed the four MPs in the region who were individual members of the T&G, to recommend sponsorship of them to the General Executive Council. This would mean part of their election expenses being paid for by the union.

All four of the MPs were questioned for about half an hour by members of the regional committee on a range of topics, including regional government, which the committee was committed to. All of the MPs satisfied the committee with their answers and they were recommended for sponsorship, which was later agreed by the GEC.

I had some worry about how the GEC would respond to Tony Blair, bearing in mind its reaction to his selection earlier in the year and the way I had ignored its views and supported Tony.

My worry was unfounded, he was unanimously supported. I knew that in the four MPs we had four strong ambassadors for devolution for the Northern region.

As expected, after the General Election in 1983, Michael Foot stood down as Leader of the Labour Party and the trade unionists were once again promoting Neil Kinnock as the potential next leader. It would seem he had little or no opposition. Neil Kinnock was something of a firebrand, an extremely good orator and, like Michael Foot, came from Wales.

The announcement of his succession to the leadership was at the Brighton Labour Party Conference in 1983. Before the announcement in the afternoon session, Moss Evans and I, Ron Todd and a couple of others went to a little pub right on the corner of the street outside the conference centre.

Ron Todd had been appointed national organiser for the T&G, having previously been a regional secretary in London. Ron was quite a good friend of Moss Evans and later took over the reins of power in the T&G when Moss retired in 1984.

We were all delighted that Neil Kinnock was the new leader, particularly because he was sponsored by the T&G. During our conversation in the pub, I suggested it might be a good idea that if, during his acceptance speech, Neil Kinnock wore a T&G tie on the platform. Both Moss and Ron thought this was a good idea.

At the time I was wearing a union tie with an N in the middle of the T&G badge. We agreed that people may think the N stood for Neil, so it was entirely appropriate for Neil Kinnock to wear my tie. Moss asked me to remove it, gave it to Ron Todd, and Ron swiftly went to the conference hall to ensure Neil Kinnock got the tie to wear during his acceptance speech when he took to the rostrum.

Neil Kinnock, ever the performer, agreed to wear the tie,

and when we got back into the conference hall it was full of newspaper reporters, photographers, television cameramen, radio reporters and television presenters from all over the world.

When the new leader of the British Labour movement stood on the platform to deliver his eloquent and passionate acceptance speech, he was given a standing ovation. And his image was beamed across the world to millions of television viewers.

I was personally delighted that the new Labour Party leader was wearing not just a T&G tie, but my tie.

The N in the middle of the T&G badge did not stand for Neil ... It stood for "Northern".

I had the ties specially made for the northern region's T&G members because the Scottish and Welsh regions all had their own personal ties with the dragon or the thistle.

After the conference, T&G members flocked to buy the ties, knowing one had been worn by the new Party Leader.

Chapter Twenty Three

Margaret Thatcher's intransigent attitude and steely determination to close the pits sparked the long and bitter miners' strike during 1984. In the same year, my family was hit by personal tragedy; the death of my father, himself a former pitman, who had problems with bronchitis and emphysema. I don't know if his health problems resulted from his work in the pit, but his years inhaling dust could never have been conducive to a healthy lifestyle.

He was taken to Chester-le-Street General Hospital before he died. I missed my father a great deal, because he was more than my father, he was a good friend. One thing I always remember about that sad time was the fact that Giles Radice, the MP for Chester-le-Street and a good friend of mine, visited my father while he lay ill in bed and spent a good hour with him talking about everything my father could relate to. My father liked Giles Radice very much and often spoke of him. He appreciated Giles' visit. I have always remembered this because it demonstrated how genuine, warm, and friendly the man is. Politicians often come under criticism for publicity seeking and doing things to catch votes. There was no publicity about his visit to my father's bedside, and there was no votes to attract

There was a great deal of activity during the miners' strike, with many demonstrations and meetings. The T&G was in total support of the miners' cause and I personally became involved and supported what they were doing. I endeavoured to raise money for the miners as often as I could , but sometimes had difficulty within my own union. Lorry drivers and bus drivers tried to breach the NUM picket lines. This infuriated the miners and I could understand why.

During the strike, one of the concessions won by the NCB was that all retired miners who received concessionary coal, as they had done for years even right back to my days as a boy in New Kyo, would continue to do so.

During my years of service with the T&G and the regional Labour Party I had some criticism of the media, but there was one incident I will never forget because of the underhand tactics involved and that was as a result of a phone call I received during the miners' strike from someone who worked for Tyne Tees Television telling me that my mother was to appear on the Tyne Tees news that night complaining about the miners' attitude towards their retired members. I was told that my mother was acting as a spokeswoman for a number of retired miners' wives in the bungalows where she lived in Bowburn. The residents were complaining that they had no coal.

On the news that night they had my mother sitting beside her fire with a small fire burning and the headline was "trade union leader supports miners while his mother sits without any coal". The news footage went on to depict my mother looking out of the window waiting for the coal man to appear. I was absolutely incensed by this coverage and phoned the television station. It seemed to me that my mother had been set up by the media to do this knocking piece.

I rang my mother and she was rather taken aback by my comments when I spoke to her. What she said was one or two of the women residents had rang Tyne Tees and mentioned her name as a person living in the same cul-de-sac. This prompted the TV crews to visit the cul-de-sac and rather than speak to the women who rang the station, they spoke to my mother and encouraged her to stand by the window, looking out for the coalman. They also suggested she held a photograph of me from her sideboard to look at for one of the shots during the piece. The whole thing, to me, was nauseating and I just couldn't believe that the media had used my mother in this way to try to have a go at the miners during the strike.

The following day I had to address a mass meeting in Stockton, along with Jack Jones and Neil Kinnock in support of the miners and, as expected, I did get a little criticism from the audience, because of my mother's attitude. I couldn't very well explain the circumstances behind her TV appearance, but I did say the media had used her.

While the miners' strike continued, in the latter part of 1984, Ron Todd, a very good friend of Moss Evans, became the General Secretary of the Transport and General Workers' Union. He took over the reins of the organisation in early 1985.

Ron Todd was a Londoner, actively involved in the motor industry, particularly Ford, before he became a national official for the union. His period in office as the General Secretary, it is my firmly-held opinion, was a disaster for the union, for the Labour Party and for the image of the trade union movement in general.

He was a populist and loved to appeal to conference through his power of oratory and he hated to be on the losing side at any conference, be it the Labour Party or TUC. Under his leadership, the extreme political interest groups enhanced their position within the union. Backstabbing, witchhunts and internal intrigue were the order of the day. During his period in office, many people told me they saw him as an actor, more interested in what he sounded like, rather than giving personal leadership.

He did not seem to realise the damage that the Tory Party was doing to the country, and did nothing at all to enhance the Labour Party's standing within the country. If he had had some of

Jack Jones' vision, image and courage he possibly could have helped the return of the Labour Government earlier. His opinions were based on conference activists' views, ignoring the mood of the people in the country who were looking for a change in administration and prepared to sacrifice to do so. He was a personable man, who liked to share jokes with leading politicians. The same politicians privately shared the view that he was doing irreparable damage to the Labour Party and to the movement, but did not have the courage to confront him because of the size of his union's block vote.

I often think about the leadership of Jack Jones, and previous to that Frank Cousins, and how the organisation had a great standing in the country and in the Labour Party. Jack Jones had the ability to conciliate and co-operate, as well as vision, to get the best possible deal for his members and trade unionists in general. This was widely recognised by everyone. Unfortunately , Jack Jones stepped down and Moss Evans took over, but due to his personal circumstances was not able to continue with the same influence as Jack Jones. Then we had the emergence of Ron Todd as the General Secretary.

I wasn't convinced at all that under his leadership we could make any inroads into the Tory majority, which was decimating the country. This concerned me because I was always looking at the problems we had within the Northern region; unemployment, social deprivation, high levels of serious health problems. We didn't seem to be able to get over them because of some of the activists within the leadership of the Labour Party and the TUC.

I wasn't thinking in terms of bowing down and accepting everything that the Conservative Party was throwing ast us, far from it, but I felt it was time that we should form alliances with other groups, such as the employers' organisations and other political parties in order to come up with something that would defeat the Tories. It wasn't considered by the leadership of the Labour Party at the time, and we paid the price with many more years of Tory rule.

Even in the northern region we were trying to establish contacts with the employers' organisations in order to try to do something about the very real problems in the region. In 1981 the TUC decided to restructure itself and create a more formal type of representation within the Northern region.

The TUC appointed a man called Bob Howard to head up the TUC in the Northern region and he was a very effective operator. He was able to introduce various structures within the region to ensure that trade unions were given proper representational rights. He established an employment policy committee, a finance committee and other types of committees, so that full debates could take place within the movement to ascertain views before making representations to the wider movement.

Over the years, Bob was very effective and extremely well liked. He became a good friend of mine.

Along with Bob Howard and the GMB regional secretary, Tom Burlison, we were able to establish a very successful event at Beamish called the Beamish Gala Day. The idea was we would ask the various trade unions to march into Beamish Museum with their banners because many of the trade unions had their roots in the days when the type of dwellings they lived in were similar to that of Beamish. We all congregated at Beamish and we had many major speakers at the Gala over the next few years. Bob worked hard to make this event a success, and it was. It received a lot of national coverage. We had Neil Kinnock and others there to put the message over to the ten or 12,000 trade union families that attended.

The event was also supported by the local authorities, and by employers who donated raffle prizes, and this tripartite approach went down very well with the communities in the North. It was this type of relationship that I was hoping could be established at national level during the next few years, but all to no avail.

Chapter Twenty Four

The closure of the pits and the shipyards in the North East had a devastating impact on the region, with the loss of thousands of jobs. Heavy industry took a real battering in the 1980s, and it became more important than ever for local authorities, unions, employers and other organisations to work together to try to attract inward investment and create more jobs.

I was asked to join the Invest In Britain Bureau, which was a body organised under the auspices of the Department for Trade and Industry. Its role, to travel the world and seek inward investment for the UK. I made several trips to parts of the world explaining the industrial relations scene in Britain and the types of relationships employers could expect to enter into with the trade unions.

I was in Japan for in more than three weeks in the mid 1980s, and was involved quite considerably, with others, with the Nissan company, trying to convince the car giant to relocate some of its operations to the UK. The Nissan company wanted a great deal of time to consider its options and the Tyne & Wear County Council was involved from the outset, along with its chief executive Jim Gardner, who did a magnificent job trying to convince the Japanese to come to the North East. The Japanese wanted to look at Wales, Humberside and the North East before they made any decision.

One of the reasons why the trade unions were endeavouring

to co-operate with the potential Nissan investment was an attempt to secure the union membership agreement. I wasn't personally interested in this aspect at all. All I wanted to try to do was to get the Nissan company in the North of England. The Nissan executive team visited Wales and the North of England and interviewed people at great length. I recall having two fairly long sessions with the Nissan group in the County Hotel, Durham, and they covered every aspect of trade union, political and economic life that I was able to offer them. A number of other people were involved in the interviews, doing a good job.

After some weeks, the Nissan company decided to locate to Washington and took the decision it would recognise the Amalgamated Engineering and Electrical Union (AEEU). This caused a lot of concern at national level within the T&G. Ron Todd was very concerned that the Nissan company had decided to recognise the AEEU rather than the T&G, after all the work that I had put in. I had to explain to him it had made its decision and there was no way at all we could breach this agreement, as the regional TUC had also given a clear lead that they would respect any decision Nissan was prepared to make. As far as I was concerned, we now had Nissan in the region. The fact that I had spent some time with Nissan and it decided to make an agreement with another union caused me no personal concern at all.

In 1985, Lirena decided to return to work and joined the theatre team at the Queen Elizabeth Hospital in Gateshead. She was able to do this because Amy – her mother – took over the role of full time nanny and did a great job with the children. She spent a great deal of time with the children while Lirena was at work and while I was travelling throughout the region and the country.

In 1985, I was also involved in a trip to Oslo, Norway, with local authority representatives, to promote the tourist attractions in Tyne and Wear. The singer from Fatfield, Alan Price, was part of our team and we had an extremely good promotional event in Oslo which I thought was a great success.

Adrian, my son, decided to emigrate to Australia in 1985 with his wife Jaqui, whom he had married two years earlier. Jaqui's mother and father had just emigrated there and her two brothers had been out there for a number of years. That helped them get established when they arrived. I was a bit concerned to see them go out there, realising it would put us out of contact. But I knew it would be good for my son and his wife to find a new life for themselves in a new country.

My other son Barry joined the Army, the Fusiliers. While in the Army he met and married a girl called Anne, from Coleraine, while he was serving in Northern Ireland, and they produced a young son, called Scott. I was delighted they gave Scott the middle name of Joseph which carried on the tradition within the Mills family. Barry and Adrian never saw each other for a number of years but Barry did go with Scott to visit Australia for four weeks and they thoroughly enjoyed themselves.

In 1985, the General Executive Council of the T&G decided to restructure its top team within the union because of several retirements, including that of Alex Kitson. The GEC decided to appoint a new Deputy General Secretary and an Executive Officer and advertised both posts. I thought long and hard about applying for the deputy's position, as I was quiet happy within my own region where I had a lot of authority and friends.

I discussed the matter with Lirena and the family and she said she would go anywhere I wanted to go to do a job on behalf of the T&G. I applied for the post and the General Executive Council decided there would be a short-list of four for the two jobs. The sub-committee of the Executive, the Finance and General Purposes Committee, decided to do the shortlisting. It came up with four names, Mal Snow, Regional Secretary in Yorkshire and Humberside, Albert Blyghton, Legal Affairs National Secretary, Larry

Smith, National Officer, and myself.

There was a lot of speculation throughout the next few weeks about who would be the successful candidate. The national daily newspapers took a great of interest in the position, knowing for a fact that the new Deputy General Secretary would eventually become the General Secretary. My name was trawled around the national media as a frontrunner for the job. I was interviewed by many journalists and told them my philosophy would be the modernisation of the union, to be more closely and politically aligned with the Labour Party, and to look at some of the outdated structures within the organisation.

I believe that the points I made to the Press might have led to my downfall. Because, when the executive met to interview the four shortlisted candidates, for the first time in the history of the T&G, it decided not to endorse the short-list that had been drawn up, preferring instead to interview all of the people who had applied for the jobs.

I went to London on a Monday morning fully expecting to be interviewed along with the three other shortlisted candidates but, after having sat there for a number of hours, we were told by Ron Todd that the executive was not prepared to endorse the short-list and that the following day all of the candidates would be interviewed. At this stage, I contemplated whether or not to pull, to refuse to go along with their decision, or to allow my name to go forward for interview.

I was contacted by a number of union friends from around the country while I was in head office and they suggested that I should go to the interview and tell the executive what my plans would be if I was to become the Deputy General Secretary. I stayed overnight in London and the following morning went into the interview. I spoke to the Executive for about half an hour and was closely questioned by them.

They were 32 members of the GEC and as I looked around

I realised it was these same individuals who had been forcing the union into precarious positions politically over the past few years. I wondered whether or not I was wasting my time. I took the full 30 minutes and explained what my intentions were and answered all the questions put to me, many of them hostile. I left the room feeling quite pleased that I had had the opportunity to speak to the Executive for half an hour and left them in no doubt about where I thought the union was going and what I would do if I got the job as Deputy General Secretary.

I am sure that my address didn't please it because, after about four hours, Ron Todd came in to tell me that the successful candidate was Bill Morris. He became the General Secretary of the union after Ron Todd retired. Eddie Hague, who was a previous national official of the Dyers' and Bleachers' Union, which had merged with the T&G, was to become the new Executive Officer.

What was odd about the situation was that none of the two candidates that had got the jobs were on the short-list agreed by the union's Finance and General Purposes Committee.

When I got on the train at Kings Cross to come home, I had a feeling of delight that I had not got the job, because I realised I would have had to move with Lirena and the two girls to London to start a new life there. I wasn't sure if I could have lived there with the job, bearing in mind the executive of the union was pursuing policies that I didn't agree with. I would have been treading a lonely path to continue in the job, if I had been appointed.

After the interviews, many people made the point to me that I had paid the price for expressing my views about the GEC's policies.

When I got home that night, Lirena and the two girls were delighted that I had not been successful, for while she had said she would have gone to London if necessary, privately Lirena was not too happy about the prospect of uprooting the family from the North.

The GEC's decision not to appoint me as Deputy General Secretary was probably one of the most important decisions to affect my life, because I went on from that date to do many other things I otherwise could not have done.

One of the things about being the principal officer of the T&G in the region, was that I was expected to attend a lot of week-long national conferences; the TUC, the T&G's biennial delegate conference, the Labour Party Conference, and others. Fortunately, Lirena was able to join me at many of these conferences, because Amy was able to look after the two girls during our absence. Sometimes Amy accompanied us on the trips.

Amy was very helpful to us, as she was with her other daughter Susan, who was a nurse and became a representative of a very large drugs company. Her first-born, Michael, had cerebral palsy and Amy spent a lot of time with Michael, who has grown up to be a bright individual with a keen interest in electronics and other recording equipment. In fact, he turned out to be a very good DJ at some of the local pubs in Newcastle. Amy, in order to support the special school Michael attended, decided on her 70th birthday to walk 70 miles from Newcastle to her birthplace in Yorkshire. She was followed daily by a Tyne Tees Television crew and was referred to in the subsequent news report as "supergran". She was an extraordinary lady and helped us considerably when the children were young.

Not all of the conferences we attended were boring. There was some rather amusing incidents that took place over the years. Like the time when my counterpart in Yorkshire and Humberside, Mal Snow, landed in Blackpool without any socks in his case and decided to go shopping. He bought six pairs for a low price and put a pair on that night. We walked quite a long way that evening. At the hotel, he came down for breakfast rather panic-stricken having found his feet were blue and swollen. He thought it was the walking we had done the previous night but when he jumped into the shower the blue hue disappeared from his feet – from the dye in the cheap socks.

There was a senior official from another union in the North walking down the street in Blackpool during the same conference who was approached by a lady who knew him. She told him her husband had gone into the gent's toilet under an underpass and she was worried he might have collapsed, as he been away quite some time. The official went into the gent's and noted there was only one toilet door closed. He went into the next cubicle and looked over the top. To his dismay there was someone else sitting on the toilet, not the woman's husband, whom he knew. The startled man on the toilet shouted: "You dirty so and so". The official walked back to the road where he saw this woman and her husband walking down the other side of the road, waving to him as if nothing had happened.

The official was to take part in a major debate during the week, but told me he had decided not to make an appearance in case he was recognised by the man who had been sitting on the toilet, who was possibly a delegate. I couldn't help but laugh.

On another occasion, I took four or five of my delegates for a meal in Blackpool in the Lancastrian Grill. We were to meet up and wait for others, having our meal at about 10.30pm. We went in and had a drink at the bar before the meal was served. The delegates – mainly dockers – were standing in the corner, putting the world to rights. Just as I was about to get the menu, Barbara Windsor and two of her friends came into the restaurant unnoticed by the docker delegates and stood next to me at the bar. I said good evening to her and started a conversation. She was appearing at one of the shows in Blackpool and was at the restaurant to celebrate the birthday of one of her colleagues. About five minutes into the conversation, Jimmy Yates, the leader of the dockers, a branch secretary from Middlesbrough, looked up and came across, and said to Barbara Windsor that he recognised her.

"Aren't you Vera Lynn?" He asked. Barbara Windsor told him to **** off and said if he was the type of delegate that was attending the TUC conference, then no wonder the country was in such a terrible state. I was terribly embarrassed by this whole episode. I apologised to Barbara and bought her and her friends a bottle of wine.

Another conference event which brought out a few laughs was during a debate on the economy. Bob Howard, who is about 5ft 6ins and has a large beard, approached me with white powder all over his beard. I thought he had been eating cake. He asked me to go to the back of the hall and there he explained to me that the General Secretary of the TUC, Norman Willis, had asked him to entertain four Russian delegates who had come over from Moscow. Bob said the Russians were dour individuals, lacking a sense of humour. Bob took them down to the Blackpool Tower Bowling Alley where he demonstrated bowling. Bob got one of the balls in his hands, had chalked his hands, was swinging it backwards and forwards, and the ball stuck to his thumb. As he bowled his top teeth came out and went flying down the middle aisle. Everyone around started laughing, apart from the Russians, as Bob walked down the centre aisle to pick up his teeth and put them back in place. This was the cause of all the white powder on his beard. I told my colleagues what had happened and we were the only delegates in the hall laughing during a serious economic debate. The television audience did pick up some responses to speeches and we were filmed laughing, but no one knew what had caused the laughter.

In late 1987, I had a very pleasant surprise joke played on me by Tyne Tees Television. I was asked to go to the studios to become involved in some programme about entertainment. I took my daughter Joanne with me and when I was shown into the studio and sat down on a chair, alongside my daughter, I was then shown a video of an old showgroup in Stanley and an old lady called Effie Herdman – formerly Wilson – who was bossing the children around, putting them on the stage and teaching them how to dance. This was the same Effie who was in charge of the showgroup when I was a young boy in New Kyo.

When the video was finished, the presenter asked me if I could still dance, and I said I could. They then played some music and I went on to perform a bit of a tap dance. Joanne took to the stage, too, and we danced together. Two minutes into the routine, I heard a voice shouting at me to lift my feet up and lift my head up and put my hands by my side while I was dancing. It was Effie who had come into the studio as part of the surprise to remind me of my days as a young dancer in New Kyo.

Effie has seen me on television several times involved in serious debates and commented to some reporter that I had been a member of her showgroup as a very young boy. This story got back to Tyne Tees, hence the suprise programme.

It went out on television that evening and suprised a lot of people. In fact it took some living down because the next time I addressed the dock workers in Middlesbrough, who were in dispute, some shouted I would far better convince them to return to work by doing a tap dance, reather than talking to them.

The Bishop of Durham, David Jenkins came to my house one day for acup of tea, after attending a meeting in Bullion Hall, and remarked how much he liked a bust of Keir Hardie I had in the hallway. He left that afternoon with the bust under arm.

"Have you been trying to convert the bishop to the Labour Party," a neighbour who saw him leave asked.

Chapter Twenty Five

The cruel closure of the shipyards, the devastating impact of the pit closures, and just when we all thought it could not worsen, along came the Poll Tax, which caused riots on the streets of Britain and turned one North East pensioner into a minor celebrity because of his refusal to pay.

Norman Laws, 71, a retired electrician, of Hebburn, South Tyneside, was jailed by magistrates in South Shields for refusing to pay his Poll Tax. He was given two months in Durham Jail. His wife, Winifred, 74, who was in poor health, had to be cared for by friends and relatives.

At the time I was visiting a number of Labour Party branches explaining my total opposition to the Poll Tax and during the demonstrations that ensued I appeared on a radio programme and was asked directly by the presenter whether I would be personally willing to pay Mr Laws' Poll Tax. I was in a bit of a corner, but replied that I would be prepared to pay his bill. The offer made the local headlines in several newspapers.

I went to Durham Prison the following day and put the deal to Norman Laws, pressing him as hard as I could. He told me he wasn't interested and that I was wasting my time. But he said there was one thing that I could do for him. Could I somehow put a stop to the flow of "happy baccy" that was being pushed under his cell door? He asked.

I told him thematter was way out of my league, but suggested he should mention it to the prison Governor. As I left the jail I was met by a posse of the media and told them I had had a long discussion with Norman Laws but he had refused to do any deals. He still was ot paying the Poll Tax. The demonstrators were delighted by his decision and I couldn't make up my mind whether Norman Laws was an awkward old so and so or a militant with high principals. As far as I remember, he served his full sentence.

In 1987, the T&G opened a brand new office building in John Dobson Street in the centre of Newcastle. The building was twice the size of the office in Barrack Road and light years away in terms of facilities The office was also to accommodate the computerisation programme for our region which we were asked to pilot. This was quite a feather in our cap.

The employees at John Dobson Street were fully equipped to deal with the computerisation, having received full training, and were able to take on more of the training progammes the union introduced. Computerisation later spread across all the offices of the T&G.

There was excellent conference and seminar facilities which were used, with my encouragement, by other organisations. The Regional Labour Party and the TUC had all their press conferences in our conference hall. This allowed me to hold meetings with the national leaders from time to time. It also gave me the opportunity to press the case for the region to have special treatment as far as jobs and economic prosperity were concerned, and to press the case for regional government to be based in the national manifesto. The John Dobson Street move was a good one and has indeed delivered quite a substantial return for the union and the Labour movement.

The Labour Party lost the 1987 General Election, even though the Tories were very unpopular. It seemed the communities were not able to trust the Labour Party because, many argued, it was full of internal strife. I think the constant arguments about defence and associated matters caused confusion in people's minds. The North of England, as usual, returned a strong Labour vote but throughout the rest of the country we didn't do that well.

I had a row with Neil Kinnock's office during the drawing up of the 1987 General Election manifesto because it was not prepared to give us a commitment to a regional development agency or regional government if Labour was elected. I indicated that if it refused to do this, I would not campaign for the party in the North. Neil Kinnock leaned on the T&G HQ to put pressure on me to change my mind. After many discussions, it agreed to put something in the manifesto which met us halfway. Not many people in the trade union and Labour movement in the North knew what was going on. Everyone simply thought Neil Kinnock had had a change of mind in his opposition to devolution, when the real reason was he wanted to avoid a big embarrassment. However, it was all to no avail because the election was lost.

Ron Todd and some of the GEC accused me of going native on the whole issue of regional government and devolution for the regions and they were not too happy with my tactics prior to the General Election.

Just before this period I became a board member of the Tyne and Wear Development Corporation. I came in for immediate flack from certain individuals within the movement. The corporation's chairman was Paul Nicholson, the chairman of Sunderland's Vaux Brewery, and the chief executive was Alistair Balls, a career civil servant. The rest of the board was made up of local businessmen and local authority representatives. These bodies were unpopular within the local authorities because they took over the planning functions of the authorities and had a lot of power, including the power to compulsorily purchase land for large developments.

I consulted widely at top level within the TUC and the

Labour movement before accepting the position and I noted that Lord Jack Dormand, the former chairman of the Parliamentary Labour Party, had been appointed to the Tees and Hartlepool Development Corporation. Colleagues suggested to me that while the Labour Party was in opposition to the principles of development corporations, it was essential that Labour movement people became involved if at all possible in order to influence decisions.

The task of the Development Corporation was substantial; to clear up the dereliction on the riverside of the Tyne and Wear and bring them into economic use. This worked very well, evidenced by the success on the river banks now. What was ironic was that many of the critics of the development corporation in the early days went on to praise its work, realising how it had enhanced the areas and provided excellent facilities for the communities.

One of my roles on the board was to provide a communication link with the local authorities, which I did regularly. I sought views on many of the proposals that the corporation was going to introduce. I found the development corporation very sensitive to local authority views.

We had a number of grand openings of facilities. One, I remember, was the opening of the Marina at St Peter's Basin in Walker, Newcastle, opened by Princess Diana, who had also agreed to open a retirement home for Walker residents nearby. Lirena and I were asked to meet the Princess on her arrival at the retirement home and show her around.

Before she arrived, she had to carry out the St Peter's ceremony. When her car arrived at the retirement home, I could see Alistair Balls, who was accompanying her, looking a bit tense. Lirena and I met Princess Diana and took her into the premises. The visit was to last 15 minutes, but it overran by 30 minutes because the Princess insisted on speaking to every resident in the home and listened to an old man playing the piano, while the rest of the residents sang to her.

This put additional pressure on the accompanying party, which didn't seem to go down very well with the Lord Lieutenant and his staff. When the Princess left, I asked Alistair Balls why he had looked so tense. He told me that when he was at the Marina she was invited aboard a yacht to have a look inside but the safety rope had prevented her from doing so. She replied she would have difficulty getting her leg over and a building worker in earshot said "I'm having the same problem myself". Sir Laurie Barratt, who was also in the accompanying party and the builder of the Marina, turned red with rage and whispered to the site foreman to find the man's name and deal with him later. It seemed that Princess Diana had just smiled at the remark and didn't seem to be offended. The matter was dropped very quickly.

When the Tyne and Wear Development Corporation was wound up, it had invested £11 million in the International Centre for Life in Newcastle for the study of genetics and to provide a visitor attraction. The Lottery Commission also made a substantial grant, as did the European Parliament. It had a lot of backers from the private sector to make it a success.

Alistair Balls took over the role as the centre's Chief Executive and Linda Conlon, head of communications at the Tyne and Wear Development Corporation, took on the job as its Corporate Affairs Director. The chairman of the International Centre for Life was Matt Ridley, a well-known science writer and the son of Lord Ridley. I was pleased to be offered the place on the new board and subsequently became the deputy chairman to Matt Ridley.

While one could see the amazing work the Tyne and Wear Development Corporation had carried out on and around the banks of the rivers Tyne and Wear, one of its lasting legacies was its major contribution to the International Centre for Life, which will go on from strength to strength.

My time on the T&W Development Corporation produced some interesting situations, none more so than when we were considering an application for the development of the former Wearmouth Colliery site as the new home for Sunderland Football Club which wanted to move from Roker Park.

Only 20 acres of the 40-acre site in north Sunderland was required for the development, which included the associated car parking spaces. It was an ideal spot for the ground, with plenty of land for further developments.

I was a member of the corporation's planning sub-committee which, along with others, was to make a decision on the development. Reclamation of potential development sites could be very expensive, depending on the typography of the land that was being reclaimed. As far as the Wearmouth Colliery development was concerned, it was a difficult site and a lot of money had to be put into reclaiming it.

It came to our attention as a planning committee that Sir John Hall, who was chairman of Newcastle United Football Club, and previously a member of the development corporation, was objecting to the development going ahead. He argued that if Sunderland Football Club was to be given planning permission, having had the land reclaimed for it, this would be an indirect subsidy to the club. I couldn't understand his argument at all, because irrespective of what end user went on that site, there would have been technically an indirect subsidy, although we did not use the term subsidy. The term was to bring into operational use derelict land, and that is what we were doing.

Sir John Hall claimed to have the interests of the North at heart. One day I was travelling by train from Newcastle to London to attend a meeting. The train stopped in Darlington and Sir John Hall got on board and sat beside me. We passed a few pleasantries, and I decided now was the opportunity for me to confront him about his views on the Wearmouth Colliery planning application. He said Newcastle United Football Club had received no grants or help from anyone, including the development corporation. Here was SAFC getting an indirect grant from the T&W Development Corporation for £8million, he argued.

I told him quite frankly that he had been a member of the development corporation and he knew what the role of the TWDC was; bringing back into economic use derelict land.

The TWDC thought the football ground would be an ideal addition to what we were doing in Sunderland. There were a further 20 acres available for other developments and I suggested to Sir John Hall that if he was interested in that 20 acres, he should put plans forward. He seemed to have some objection to the mere fact that Sunderland Football Club would get some benefit.

The Stadium of Light was built, and it is a superb addition to the Sunderland landscape. A magnificent ground standing right on the banks of the River Wear with a lot of access for fans. The other 20 acres will be developed in due course.

The whole episode with Sir John Hall made me a little annoyed to think that a man with his profile, who always appeared to support the region, would try and engage in arguments to stop what I thought was an excellent development for Sunderland Football Club.

As well as my involvement with the TWDC, the International Centre for Life, and other organisations, I was still very much involved with the Labour Party.

One of the most enjoyable nights at the Labour Party conference was the Geordie Night, which had been going on for many years. A number of Northern delegates took the view that at Labour Party conferences, we always had the Welsh, Scottish and

Irish nights, with nothing organised for the regions. So we decided to organise the Geordie Night and bring down to conference some of the regional and national stars from the North East.

The driving force behind this initial proposal was Joyce Quinn, the MP for Gateshead and Washington West. We organised our first Geordie Night at the Tangerine Club in Blackpool, the social club for the Blackpool Football Club, and it was a magnificent success. Alan Hull, the lead singer in Lindisfarne, the comedian Mike Elliott, and others provided the entertainment.

We started the Geordie Night off in a very small and informal way, but as the years progressed, it became a national event in the Labour Party calendar, and the Leader of the Labour Party and various shadow ministers always put in an appearance. It was such a success that we were approached by the leader's office which suggested that we switch the evening from a Tuesday night to a Wednesday night. The Leader of the Labour Party always gives his keynote speech on a Wednesday afternoon at conference and this restricted him from enjoying himself at the Geordie Night. He needed a clear head. We agreed to switch it from a Tuesday to Wednesday evening. The Geordie Night continues to be a major success.

Chapter Twenty Six

The ordinary members of the Labour party, the foot soldiers who did so much work during the local and national elections, kept the party alive. But what they did not have was a say, as an individual, on the selection of prospective parliamentary candidates. I had always felt this was wrong and, after the Labour Party lost the 1987 General Election, I thought then was an opportune time to try to do something to change this undemocratic process.

The T&G's biennial delegate conference was held at Scarborough, North Yorkshire, in 1987. This was when almost 1,000 delegates from the union would come together to discuss motions submitted by the branches, covering anything from general economics to T&G policies. On the agenda at Scarborough there would be about 900 motions, many of which would be composited in order to get them on the agenda for debate.

I had a discussion with my union's regional committee in the North and it was agreed we would put a motion on the agenda for the Scarborough conference suggesting that the selection of prospective parliamentary candidates within constituencies should be on the basis of one-member, one-vote

By far, the trade union delegates outnumbered the ordinary branch members in the Constituency Labour Parties (CLPs) and lots of unions affiliated as many delegates as they could to the CLP in order to ensure they had a major say in who it was who became the parliamentary candidate.

My colleagues and I in the North spoke to a number of our friends around the country to see if we could get some support from their areas. I spoke to Mal Snow, the Regional Secretary of the Yorkshire and Humberside area, who had similar feelings to myself on this issue and he felt that his delegates would support the motion. John Joynson, the south west Regional Secretary of the T&G, who was based in Bristol, thought the motion should be supported but realised there could be some resistance. We made a few other inquiries to interested parties across the country, some were sympathetic, others were extremely hostile.

When the agenda was published for the biennial delegate conference, the motion was numbered 399, and it stuck out like a sore thumb. Naturally, the media picked this motion up and a great deal of interest was engendered throughout the union and Labour movements. Left-wing interests were inevitably hugely resistant to change; in fact they were up in arms that the motion had made it on to the agenda at all. If the biennial conference could change this policy, then the union would try to influence the Labour Party to do the same. One large union with a block vote in excess of 1,750,000 members would have a big influence.

I realised, and so did my regional committee, that we would have a lot of opposition from the extreme left within the union. I knew that a lot of union members who attended the conference were not members of the Labour Party but other political fringe groups. I was strongly of the view that only Labour Party members of the T&G should really have a say in how the democratic processes operated within the party, but I realised we could not impose this on the biennial delegate conference, because it was a trade union conference.

We had to hatch a plan on how we would deal with the motion when it came up on the agenda. Some weeks before the conference, I approached Lillian Kennedy, a delegate from a company in Newcastle, who was very active within the Labour Party and the trade union branch. She was also a member of my regional committee and district committee and active throughout the North in the union's womens' section. I asked her if she would be prepared to move the motion at the biennial conference, knowing how controversial it would be, and she readily agreed.

Knowing my view about the ordinary Labour members having some positive say in how the Labour Party democracy should work, we came up with the tactic that when Lillian went to the platform to deliver her speech in support of the motion, she should have some blue tack on the back of her Labour Party card which she would attach to the rostrum. This would give an opportunity for delegates to challenge subsequent speakers who may be in opposition to the motion. This was a tactic to help us smoke out the other fringe groups who may have tried to bounce the conference in another direction. If you can shout from the body of the hall, "are you a member of the Labour Party and where is your card", it would distract anti-Labour Party speakers.

On the day the motion was taken, the conference hall in Scarborough was crawling with various fringe groups with leaflets and other publications telling the delegates to oppose motion 399. The leaflets also accused the Northern region of being under the influence of right-wingers.

The conference started and, as planned, Lillian Kennedy went to the rostrum, pinned her Labour Party card to it, and delivered a very powerful speech, explaining she was a member of the Labour Party and proud to be so and she felt that, as an individual, she should have a say in the selection of parliamentary candidates

A very acrimonious debate followed and a lot of venom was spewed out by delegates.

At the end of the debate, Ron Todd had to wind up the

various points within the motion and I could see that he wasn't very happy that motion 399 appeared to have a lot of support. When the vote was taken, motion 399 supporting further democratisation within the Labour Party was passed by a small majority. The arguments on this spilled over into the coffee rooms and the pubs afterwards, and well into the night.

The Press reported the outcome and it looked as though the T&G would have to now influence some changes within the Labour Party, because the biennial delegate conference, the supreme policy-making body of the union, before any other union had even considered the very thorny subject of one-member, one-vote, had volunteered these changes. I was personally delighted that the move had now taken place and hoped other unions would follow the T&G's lead. I realised, however, that there was still a lot of manoeuvring going on behind the scenes.

My elation to these changes, which I thought would affect the whole of the Labour Party, was short-lived.

A week later when we went to London, the regional and national secretaries had a post-conference debriefing. Ron Todd went through the various motions that would affect the union's policies in the future and when he came to motion 399, he said that in his wind-up speech he had suggested there were some reservations about this policy and therefore the matter would be again debated by the General Executive Council. I was absolutely furious and I stood up and said that, as far as I was concerned, the biennial delegate conference was the supreme policy-making body of the union, and the resolution was quite simple, it asked for the selection of parliamentary candidates to be chosen on the basis of one- member, one-vote. For Ron Todd to suggest that the GEC had to examine the issue again was tantamount to ignoring the conference policy. I suggested he was wrong to do so. With one or two notable exceptions, the rest of the regional and national secretaries just sat on their hands appearing to agree with Ron Todd's view. I couldn't believe my ears and when the meeting closed I hopped back on the train to Newcastle feeling very let down by Ron Todd. It wasn't a complicated motion, it was quite simple and it had been passed at conference. It should have been the T&G's policy and should have been made clear to the Labour Party conference in Brighton that year.

The following day I rang Mal Snow and, like me, he couldn't believe what was happening. The decision of the biennial conference could have prompted the T&G to take the high ground to promote a debate within the Labour Party to start the democratisation process within its ranks, but it had failed to do so. Had this process started in 1987 the Labour Party's standing in the country may have changed considerably over the next few years. But it didn't. A great chance was missed.

In 1989, Lirena and I decided the four of us should visit Adrian and Jaqui in Australia on a three-week trip, stopping at Singapore and Bangkok on the return journey. We organised this through the Quantus group. We had a wonderful time and during our stay in Australia I had a pre-arranged meeting with the Premier of Western Australia, Peter Dowding. The meeting had been arranged by Peter Mandelson, the MP for Hartlepool. The reason for the meeting was to speak about the logistics of decentralised Government, its benefits and its drawbacks.

The meeting with Peter Dowding lasted a couple of hours and it was helpful to my thinking about devolved Government. Before he left, he asked me if I wanted to meet some union leaders during my visit. Although this was a family holiday, I didn't think my family would mind me meeting some of my counterparts in Australia.

Three days later, I received an invitation to a special reception in the public services union HQ to meet general secretaries and presidents from different unions, including the transport union. I made some useful contacts which I used to good purpose in later years.

It was these contacts I used when I tried to assist Ian Clarke, the agent for the Bank of England in Newcastle, in trying to trace his daughter Caroline who went missing while backpacking in Australia. Unfortunately, she was found murdered in the bush, causing the family a great deal of distress and unhappiness. The transport union members in Australia had carried pictures of Caroline in their cabs.

Chapter Twenty Seven

Shorty after our holiday in Australia we moved from Picktree Lodge Cottage in Chester-le-Street to Beamish Drive in Washington, in a cul-de-sac where we met some of the friendliest neighbours I have ever encountered. We got on extremely well and remain good friends to this day.

In 1992, my mother died in Shotley Bridge Hospital in Stanley. She had lived on her own in Bowburn since my father had died and missed him considerably. Although I visited once a week, and made many phone calls to her, I realised she wasn't managing that well. After a few months, I thought it would be a good idea for her to move into a residential care home, so she could have full time care. I came to that conclusion after I visited her house one day and found that a tea towel had been singed. The mere fact she was still using a coal fire also concerned me. I spoke to my Aunt Meggie, who now lived in Stanley, and she said that there was a care home not far from where she lived, run by Durham County Council, and a place could be secured for my mother there.

I made the inquiries to Durham County Council and it agreed to offer her a place. My mother eventually agreed to the move when she found out it was near Meggie and only five or six miles up the road from me then in Chester-le-Street.

She stayed in the home for 12 months but her mind started to deteriorate and she became very unhappy. The last time I saw mother alive was when I went to visit her one day. She seemed terribly distressed and I asked her what the problem was and she just said she was unhappy and she was getting all sorts of chest pains. I suggested to the matron that a doctor should be sent for, and this was done. When we left my mother she came to the window and waved us goodbye and we departed for home. Within two hours we got a call from the home to say that she had been taken to hospital.

We rushed to the hospital to find that she had suffered a heart attack. She only lasted for about two days and died on August 22nd, 1992, 11 years after my father passed away on June 5th, 1981.

My last trade union organised trip was supposed to be to Israel to see how the Palestinians were faring under the Israeli occupation. The visit had been organised by the regional TUC's Bob Howard after discussions with the PLO, whose representative, Joseph Allen, was a regular attender at the Labour Party and TUC conferences. I was a member of the Labour Friends of Israel group as well as the Labour Friends of Palestine, and while I had received lots of information about the Israeli case, I wasn't fully au fait with what was happening in Palestine, particularly on the West Bank.

The TUC thought it was a good idea to undertake a visit to the area and talk to some of the trade union leaders about the occupation. The arrangements were made and we went to Gatwick to depart on a flight to Israel. Unfortunately, the El Al security people decided that we needed to be closely questioned about our intentions. There was initially four of us on the delegation, but we were joined by two more people, an activist in the trades council movement on Teesside, and his friend, who was a photographer. I was accompanied by three of my colleagues from the executive of the TUC.

We were asked why we wanted to go the West Bank and

we explained we were a TUC delegation purely and simply on a fact-finding tour. We would come back, assimilate information, and pass it on to our members so they would have some information about what was going on. This didn't satisfy the security people vetting the passengers, and we were subjected to about three hours of close interrogation.

The question constantly being asked was were we travelling as a group rather than individuals? I answered yes, not realising the significance of the question. After about four hours in total we were told we would not be able to fly, that the aircraft was taking off, and we would not be able to board. I couldn't understand this and asked why we weren't being allowed to travel. The security people refused to give us a proper answer. Our plight was reported on the national and regional television news, which was quite an embarrassment.

Lirena was expecting me to call her that night from Israel, but she saw on the news that our party had been stopped at Gatwick Airport. She got the impression that we had been deemed some kind of security risk.

We all made formal complaints during the next few days. Two weeks later we were advised by the Israeli authorities that two of the party who had joined us at Gatwick had been to Palestine previously and had been giving out leaflets to various groups. I then realised that when I was asked if we were travelling as a group, if I had said no, we would probably have been allowed to fly.

In 1993, we saw the fourth election defeat of the Labour Party, which devastated everyone in the movement. We had hoped to make some inroads into Tory seats, but all to no avail.

Union membership across the country generally was reducing and many of the trade unions were finding themselves in financial difficulties.

It was quite apparent to us all that since Thatcher had

come to power in 1979 she had made it her intention to have a frontal assault on the trade union movement. Her policies of rationalisation and privatisation had this effect, and lots of people were no longer keen on maintaining their union membership, as they feared it could jeopardise their job prospects.

As a regional secretary for the T&G, I found that the union organisers were having little or no success attracting new members. In fact, we were incurring a regular monthly loss, which affected our income.

Ron Todd retired as the General Secretary of the T&G that year and, as had been widely predicted, Bill Morris became the boss of the union, with a major task of sorting out the organisation ahead of him

At the time, I felt that had we been a little more co-operative and understanding in the Labour Party since the 1979 election, rather than having the full frontal assaults and ranting tirades at our conferences, things may have been different. The outgoing General Secretary, Ron Todd, played a major part in making it absolutely clear that the T&G was not prepared to compromise on any of its principles or objectives, all of which appeared to me to be in direct conflict with many of the views, aspirations and desires expressed by many within the Labour Party and, it appeared, in the community at large. The Labour Party and the unions were seen as being the cause of many of the economic problems in Great Britain. This was, of course, untrue because Mrs Thatcher's policies were devastating the communities. She had wrecked many industries, including shipbuilding, engineering and coal mining, and the result was once again high unemployment across the country, felt more sharply in the Northern region than elsewhere.

Nevertheless, the electorate seemed to think that the trade unions had been to blame for some of the problems.

Within a few weeks of Bill Morris taking office, he engaged a number of management consultants to look at the union from the top to the bottom and to examine all of its structures. He indicated to the regional secretaries that this was an open book consultation period and that there would be no predetermined position taken by him as the T&G's General Secretary. I wasn't sure or not to accept this view and became a bit suspicious when rumours started to go around the union that Bill Morris was going to reduce the number of regions throughout the country.

I believed if this was to happen, the General Executive Council would in no way want to get rid of the Northern region, because of its geographical position and its strong and historic association with the trade union movement and the Labour Party. That view was short-lived. It emerged that mergers would take place, including the two Yorkshire regions and the Northern region. This rumour got to the staff of the T&G within the Northern region and they started a campaign to save it. Bill Morris was very annoyed at this campaign and he strongly believed that I was the motivational force behind it.

My colleague in Yorkshire, Mal Snow, had the same vibes from his discussions, as did my colleague in the south west John Joynson. It was perhaps no coincidence that the three regions which would be affected by the rumoured shake-up were headed by three outspoken regional secretaries who were not always in accord with the General Executive Council's views. We had to wait until the consultant's report was produced.

One of the things that concerned me about the whole scenario was that in the North of England a number of large organisations had left the Newcastle area and had moved their headquarters to Leeds, including the Conservative Party. It was rumoured also that the Labour Party may move its regional HQ to Leeds. I thought that this would be a bad signal to give people in the North.

I was in the position of being unable to criticise the banks and insurance companies who were also moving their headquarters from Newcastle, if the Northern regional office of the T&G was to go the same way. I was also concerned about the effect this would have on our arguments for regional government and devolution. I couldn't see a situation where we could sustain a good argument for devolution for the Northern region if the boundaries of the region were to include Yorkshire. It was becoming clear to many of us that while we had strong views about our region, these weren't shared by people at the top of the T&G.

When the consultant's report was produced and considered by the GEC it proposed that the Yorkshire and Northern regions should merge, which would mean it was covering an area stretching from Berwick in the north to Peterbrorough in the south. This didn't make any sense to me at all. The traditional economic boundaries of the country had been ignored.

The GEC also proposed to merge two regions in the south west.

It was quite clear from the GEC that the job of new regional secretaries for the newly-merged regions would be open to applicants for interview.

Despite my deep reservations about the new enlarged regions, I decided I would have to indicate an interest in the post of Northern and Yorkshire Regional Secretary.

However, knowing the way the GEC worked, and its political complexion, I knew in my heart of hearts that my career in the T&G was about to come to an end.

I reflected on the many arguments I had had with the GEC on some of its policies and stances it had taken within the TUC and the Labour Party; my decision not to tow the party line in the selection of a candidate for Sedgefield by supporting Tony Blair rather than Les Huckfield; my push, the first push by any union leader, for one-member, one-vote in the Labour Party, and the many other smaller issues where my philosophies and those of the GEC were at loggerheads.

This really was game, set and match to the GEC and to the General Secretary of the T&G, Bill Morris.

It didn't take too long for Bill Morris to put the proposals for the mergers to the GEC and to a special rules conference. The regions were reduced from eleven to eight. Rumours then became rife throughout the T&G, and in the wider trade union movement, about who would get the new regional secretaries' jobs.

My view was that this was no longer about a person's ability to do the job or their ability to lift the profile of the organisation across the regions, it was all about personalities. I had been critical of the union for a long time and while it could be argued that I had been disloyal to the T&G's policies, I believed it was my fundamental right to tell the executive, or anyone within the organisation prepared to listen, that I believed its policies were wrong. I was not prepared to be gagged.

My two colleagues John Joynson, in the south west, and Mal Snow in Yorkshire, held similar views and when the speculation went on about who was to be displaced from the regional posts there was only ever three names in the frame; Mills, Snow and Joynson.

At the time all this was going on, I had to attend a meeting in Brussels for the TUC with Bob Howard, the regional TUC secretary. I didn't feel much like attending, but the northern region had set up an office in Brussels to promote the North in Europe and we had to meet a number of important contacts to try to improve the employment situation in the region in the hope of attracting inward investment.

When I arrived back in Newcastle from Brussels, I received a tannoy message at the airport asking me to contact Lirena at the Queen Elizabeth Hospital in Gateshead without delay. This caused me a great deal of concern and worry because I knew she had an appointment with a consultant at the hospital. I lost no time in contacting her and she advised me to go to the hospital urgently.

When I got there she was with our good friend and neighbour Sandra Golightly and she told me she had been diagnosed with a life-threatening illness. My mind went numb and I didn't not what to say. I looked at her and told her everything would be OK. It was the only thing I could think of saying. It was a very tearful occasion and we discussed with the consultant, Bill Cunliffe, when he could operate on Lirena. Plans were put into place very quickly. I was pleased that Bill Cunliffe with the help of another surgeon, Neil McLean, from Newcastle General Hospital, had agreed to carry out the operation because, apart from the fact that he worked with Lirena as a colleague, he knew her very well. I was extremely worried about her but now knew it was in the hand of God and two excellent surgeons.

The eight-hour operation took place within a few days and I was told it had gone as well as could be expected. Two days later, I had to attend a meeting with the members of the GEC in London to convince them that I was the man for the new job, realising of course that their minds had already been made up.

When I entered the T&G's headquarters in London I was worried stiff about Lirena and felt that I should really have really been at her bedside, rather than preparing to go through with this mockery of an interview.

When I entered the chamber of the GEC, I was welcomed by Bill Morris who asked me to address the council about my aspirations and desires for the union if I was to become the new regional secretary in the enlarged region.

Slowly, I stood up, looked around the executive chamber and saw a lot of members shuffling papers. None of them had the courage to look me in the eye. I decided that this was the opportunity I had been waiting for, for many years.

Knowing that I wasn't going to get the job, I decided to give them a piece of my mind.

I told them where I stood on many issues, views which were diametrically opposed to those of the GEC. I also said that the Labour Party was in the wilderness because of trade union policies, which had, in turn, allowed the Tories into power. I explained that how in the Northern region we had the highest unemployment in mainland Britain and this had been with us for many years. I told them I believed the union should have been more collaborative with employers and more co-operative with the Labour Party, and if it had been that way, we could possibly have had a Labour Government in power, addressing some of the major problems we were now facing.

When I finished and sat down, the silence in that imposing hall was deafening. I asked if the executive members had any questions. A few questions were asked about informal issues, not relevant to the points that I had made at all. Bill Morris thanked me for my address and I then left the chamber. When I closed the door behind me I knew that I had closed the door on a career spanning 29 years.

I got the train back to Newcastle and went straight to the hospital to see Lirena. She was covered in all sorts of wires and tubes. When I saw her lying in the bed, I realised where my priorities lay. She asked me how the interview had gone and I told her that it had gone the way I had anticipated; a farce. The job was given to one of my colleagues from Yorkshire, Mike Davey, who was a nice man who I knew had been very effective in his region. I'm sure that when he did take the job as the new regional secretary of the expanded northern region, he was just the person the General Executive Council was looking for.

I had a feeling that a great weight had been lifted from my shoulders, and when I sat with Lirena and held her hand, we talked about her problems and how we would work together for ourselves, our family and our friends. As I held her hand, I looked to the right of the bed and there was a large basket of flowers. I leaned over and pulled out the card. The flowers were from Bill Morris, wishing her a speedy recovery with best wishes from him and the General Executive Council. I thought this was rather poignant and we both looked at each other and realised the message possibly had more significance than we had first realised.

My main priority now was to ensure that Lirena was nursed back to health.

Chapter Twenty Eight

My departure form the T&G's northern regional office resulted in me receiving many letters, some from MPs, the CBI and local employers, offering their commiserations. One of the nicest letters I received was from S&N Breweries. Gavin Reed, the company's vice-chairman, who asked me to attend a lunch to meet the directors as a kind of token of appreciation for my involvement with the company over the years. Strange, I thought I had always been a thorn in their side.

When I got to the lunch many of the directors I had dealt with over the years were present. We had a very pleasant meal and afterwards Gavin lifted up a crate of Newcastle Brown Ale and presented it to me as a thank-you from the company for my service. He took one of the bottles from the crate and on the label was a picture of myself next to the blue star. This was a tremendous honour for me, to have my picture emblazoned on a bottle of brown ale. Gavin gave me a number of the labels that he had specially printed for me, so I could distribute them to friends.

My other activities kept me very busy when I left the union. But I wasn't quite ready to dispose of my union negotiating skills.

I spent a lot of time with the Industrial Diseases Compensation company, formed by Dave Towler, a colleague of mine from the TUC executive days. Dave had been employed in the Unemployment Centre in Sunderland and did a tremendous amount of work for people, particularly those with industrial injuries and problems with the DSS. Dave decided to leave the centre to set up his own company to deal with this on a national basis. The company changed its name from Industrial Disease Compensation Ltd to Freeclaim IDC, and has been very successful.

It was through my involvement with this company, a number of years after leaving my post as the T&G's regional secretary, that I helped to bring an end to the longest-running industrial dispute in the country at Magnet Joinery in Darlington.

Ian Drysdale, a founder member of IDC, told me he knew the owner of Magnet Joinery socially and that the dispute, which had been going on for more than a year and had been infiltrated by outside political interest groups, had hit a stale-mate.

The strike was having a devastating effect on the families involved and on the town of Darlington. It was also having an impact on the efforts in attracting inward investment to the North East.

I met the owner of the company and told him every dispute had to come to an end eventually, and the longer the dispute lasted, the harder it would be to find a solution. After our meeting, and many telephone conversations, he agreed to re-open negotiations with the union, but said the company did not want to make the approach. I made the approach to one of my former union colleagues, meetings took place, and the dispute eventually came to an end. For some time I had acted as a kind of invisible intermediary.

I also spent a lot of time with the University of Northumbria in Newcastle as deputy chairman of the governors and a member of various sub-committees. I found the enthusiasm within the university electrifying and I thoroughly enjoyed working with everyone there.

I also spent some time with the International Centre for Life, as deputy chairman of trustees. This, again, is a growing concern and is becoming successful under the chairmanship of Matt Ridley and Alistair Balls, its chief executive.

In 1994, I attended my last regional Labour Party Conference in Darlington, and it was quite an emotional event. The delegates attended from different parts of the region to debate many issues and once again the question of regional government dominated the agenda. It was quite clear from the conference that we had been trying to pursue this issue for many years but only if Labour were in Government would there be any chance of achieving our aims for regional government.

At the conference, the Leader of the Labour Party, John Smith, presented me with a gift for my service to the Labour Party and to the T&G and made some extremely kind comments about my service with both.

I looked around at the conference hall and realised this would be the last time I would be chairing this body which I had chaired for 14 years. I also realised that many of the things we had debated over the years had not yet been achieved. One of them being the issue of regional government.

I spoke to Derek Foster, the MP for Bishop Auckland who had been Parliamentary Private Secretary to Neil Kinnock from 1993 to 1995 and Chief Whip from 1985 to 1995, after the conference and said that I hoped that when we had a Labour Government returned, it would deliver all the promises for the region we had debated over the years.

We had many of the leading lights from the Labour Party in the North in the Shadow Cabinet who would no doubt want to deliver for the region. Derek looked at me and said the first thing we needed to do was to ensure we had the return of a Labour government.

Derek, who has been a great friend to me and my family for many years, realised, of course, that it wasn't just as simple as I was hoping. Firstly, you had to achieve power and then you had to have the determination and the drive to bring about the changes for the Northern region that were needed.

Unfortunately, in 1994 we had the tragic death of John Smith, who suffered a massive heart attack. John was greatly missed by many people within the Labour movement because he was a very serious and honest broker. Many people had a tremendous amount of confidence in him and looked forward to him becoming Prime Minister.

Tony Blair became the Leader of the Labour Party shortly after John's death, although there were some within the party who suggested that Gordon Brown should have been his natural successor. I was delighted that Tony Blair had become Leader, not only because of my personal friendship and association with him, but because I realised that if he did become the next Prime Minister, we would have a very strong voice in the North.

In the same year, I was offered and accepted the chairmanship of the NHS Trust in Sunderland Priority Healthcare Wearside, which is a mental health and community trust, and I enjoyed the job very much. Two years later, I became the chairman of Sunderland Health Authority, a job that I enjoyed for a period of almost seven years.

What I didn't realise, because of the constant demand on the services of health professionals and insufficient funding to meet those demands, was that the politics within the NHS could be more severe than the some of the problems I had been associated with over the years in the T&G and in the Labour movement.

I was given the opportunity to represent the NHS on the regional assembly in the North East after I became chairman of the health authority. This was quite ironic because I was now debating the problems of the region from a health perspective rather than a political perspective. My colleagues realised that with all of my experience in the political arena, I could contribute to the debate from all angles.

I was still a member of the Port of Tyne Authority, on which I served for 25 years (its longest-serving board member) and I witnessed its changing fortune over time; from losing the iron ore traffic when the Consett Iron Company closed to it obtaining the Nissan contract – a contract for the importing and exporting of Nissan parts and cars to and from a roll-on, roll-off ferry site in South Shields. What a turn-around that was, and I feel proud to have been involved in both attracting Nissan to Wearside and to being involved in the Port of Tyne securing the Nissan contract.

When I left the union in 1993 and the Labour Party in 1994, I didn't really think that the things that I had been involved in over the years would be recognised in some way. I wasn't looking for recognition at all. I was just wanting to get on with the job of improving the economic prosperity of the North and to achieve some of the things that I thought about as a young man.

However in 1993, the University of Teesside decided to give me an honorary degree, a Master of Law, for my work within the Northern region and the wider trade union movement. This was followed by a Doctor of Law honorary degree from Sunderland University for my work within the region on inward investment and the trade union and Labour movement.

In 1995, I received an honorary MBA from the University of Northumbria for my work within the union, the Labour Party and the Northern region. I was advised by my friends that this was the first time that a Northerner had received three honorary degrees from three universities within such a short space of time.

Our two daughters, Joanne and Lucy, both graduated. Lucy with a BA (Hons) degree in Business and Marketing from the University of Lincolnshire and Humberside and Joanne with a degree in Law from the University of Northumbria. The girls worked very hard and their mother and I feel extremely proud of them both.

The ultimate recognition given to me was an OBE,

awarded to me in 1995 for my work within the T&G union and within the community. I was absolutely delighted to be given this award because, as far as I was concerned, it was not only recognition for myself but also my family.

When I received the OBE, Lirena, Joanne and Lucy travelled to London and stayed in a good hotel overnight. Derek Foster was able to organise a limousine to take us to the Palace.

We entered the Palace and I felt very proud that here was a boy from New Kyo about to receive an award from Prince Charles. My wife and two daughters were asked to go to another part of the Palace for guests and I was then directed into the room where all the award winners were congregating.

Within half an hour, we were assembled at the rear of the large hall and Prince Charles was about to commence the ceremony. While this was happening, the band of the Guards played in the background and my mind raced back to my days at Royal Windsor. I was escorted towards Prince Charles, who pinned the award on me, and a citation was read out about my services to the community and to the Transport and General Workers' Union.

As I walked back to my place, I thought of my upbringing in New Kyo, my dreams of doing something worthwhile, and I reflected on why I was standing in the grand and opulent surroundings of Buckingham Palace, with one of the country's highest awards pinned on my lapel.

Had all those dreams I had as a young man on making a difference to other people's lives through the influential positions I had held over the years, become reality? Had life improved in New Kyo?

With my OBE, and all of the other awards I had received, I had achieved something for myself, personally.

But my burning desire to see changes for the better in the lives of people in the North of England, I knew, remain unfulfilled.

The streets of New Kyo were virtually the same.

Over the years I had constantly pressed the case for special treatment for the North to deal with its underlying problems. The only way forward for the North is through self-determination in the form of regional government.

We can't wait another 40 years; the problems need to be addressed now.

I remember my discussions with many people over the years; people on their way to achieving high government office, and I remember the debates we had and the commitment they showed to the North.

I hope they, too, remember our discussions.